To my father, Corporal Arthur Fred Price,
"a real hero . . . who never came back."

REAL HEROES:

Rutherford County Men
Who Made the Supreme Sacrifice
During World War II

Anita Price Davis

Published by The Honoribus Press
Post Office Box 4872
Spartanburg, South Carolina 29305

Printed in the United States of America

Altman Printing Company, Inc.

Please contact Anita Price Davis if you have other information or photographs for a future edition of *Real Heroes: Rutherford County Men Who Made the Supreme Sacrifice During World War II.*

Dr. Anita Price Davis
Box 72
Ellenboro, NC 28040
828-453-7381 (Home)
anita13@charter.net

Dr. Anita Price Davis
Converse College
Spartanburg, SC 29302
864-596-9085 (Work)

DEDICATION

Real Heroes*: Rutherford County Men Who Made the Supreme Sacrifice During World War II is dedicated to the memory of my father, Corporal Arthur Fred Price, whose pleasant disposition earned him the name "Happy." *Real Heroes* is a reminder of him, his life, and his sacrifice.

A total of 149 service men from Rutherford County sacrificed their lives between December 7, 1941, and December 31, 1945. *Real Heroes*: Rutherford County Men Who Made the Supreme Sacrifice During World War II* is also a tribute to them and to their sacrifice. Hopefully, *Real Heroes* will help us not to forget those who gave their lives–"real heroes."

Contact me if you have other information or photographs for a future edition of *Real Heroes: Rutherford County Men Who Made the Supreme Sacrifice During World War II.*

---

*John Henry Bradley, who participated in the best-known flag raising on Iwo Jima during World War II, remarked, "The real heroes. . .are the guys who didn't come back." (Bradley, James. *Flags of Our Fathers*. New York: Bantam Books, 2000, p. 4)

None of these 149 men from Rutherford County came back. I chose, therefore, to call this book *Real Heroes!*

In GRATEFUL MEMORY OF

Corporal Arthur F. Price, A.S.No. 34778984,

WHO DIED IN THE SERVICE OF HIS COUNTRY AT

in the European Area, December 28, 1944.

HE STANDS IN THE UNBROKEN LINE OF PATRIOTS WHO HAVE DARED TO DIE

THAT FREEDOM MIGHT LIVE, AND GROW, AND INCREASE ITS BLESSINGS.

FREEDOM LIVES, AND THROUGH IT, HE LIVES

IN A WAY THAT HUMBLES THE UNDERTAKINGS OF MOST MEN

Franklin D Roosevelt

PRESIDENT OF THE UNITED STATES OF AMERICA

ACKNOWLEDGMENTS

This book is not the work of one person. Many people deserve credit. On each biography I have tried to identify specific persons who helped. There are others, however, who have been particularly instrumental in the completion of this work.

First, James R. Brown, publisher of *The Daily Courier,* purchased rights to several local newspapers, including *The Forest City Courier, The Spindale Sun,* and *The Rutherford County News.* He gave me permission to quote freely from the papers and to use the photographs. Without these historical records, I could not have completed this work. He ran notices in *The Daily Courier* about the upcoming book. His graciousness and his help will never be forgotten.

Converse College–my employer–encouraged and helped me in this endeavor.

Third, Brigadier General Ed. Y. Hall collaborated with me about this work from its beginning and served as an editor and a friend.

Jim Bishop of WCAB announced that I was welcoming information and photographs. After his interview of me, I received 30 calls, including William Deviney, Joyce Hutchins, and others whom I have acknowledged throughout the book. I thank him and WCAB.

Jerrell Bedford advised, photographed, proofed, emailed, gave driving directions, expressed interest, and generally encouraged. I thank him immensely.

Wanda Costner Robbins expended time and effort in helping to trace the living relatives of many of these men–particularly those from Tri-High School. She placed many calls and even picked up a photograph for me.

James M. Walker of Ellenboro contributed his time, his expertise, his photographic skills, his enthusiasm, his editing skills, his materials, and his meticulous record keeping to the task.

Nancy and Harold Stallcup shared their records with me. Edward

Price, Falls Price, Boyce Grindstaff, Guy Morehead, Reba Hamrick, Jessie Gibbs, Walda Carpenter, John Brooks, E. J. McKeithan, Sue Toms, and the staffs of the Mooneyham Public Library, the Isothermal Community College Library, and the Mickel Library volunteered information that was priceless. Dena Gomez and Juanita Pesaro contributed their skills. Friends, coworkers, and family listened–and listened–and listened.

Carolyn Grindstaff Barbee contributed recollections, photographs, memorabilia, interest, books, and love. I rejoice in our renewed friendship.

Louise Hunt scanned, printed, and accompanied me on several trips to find materials. Louise kept telling me to "slow down"; sometimes I heeded. . .

My gratitude goes to my loving son Robert, my wonderful daughter-in-law Stacey, and my husband Buren Davis. They are always accepting of my projects and my work. Without their help in so many ways, I could not have completed this task. I give them my thanks and my love.

Anita Price Davis
Ellenboro, North Carolina
April 2002

Anita Price Davis (author), Robert Eric and Stacey C. Davis (her son and daughter-in-law), and Buren Lee Davis (her husband).

TABLE OF CONTENTS

FOREWORD

On Sunday, December 7, 1941, the Japanese attack on Pearl Harbor rocked the nation. The following day, President Franklin D. Roosevelt predicted that December Seventh "would live in infamy." After his speech, the United States formally declared war against the Empire of Japan. This conflict developed into a world war–World War II.

World War II "hit Rutherford County like a great blight." (Griffin, p. 18) A total of over 5,000 men from the county took part in the war; this number was over 12 percent of the total population of the county. The sacrifice made by Rutherford County was far above its "fair" share.

> Nothing else had ever approached these figures, except in the days of the Civil War when about sixteen percent of the population was engaged in the conflict, which led one Confederate official to remark that the seed corn of the South was being used in that conflict. Of the 21 counties of western North Carolina, Rutherford had furnished the second largest number of men . . . excelled only by Buncombe [a county with three times the population of Rutherford County]. (Griffin, pp. 18-19)

North Carolina had 361,000 people who served in the military during World War II. Five thousand of these were from Rutherford County. This was about 1% of the total of the state; based on the fact that there were 100 counties in North Carolina, that was not an unreasonable percentage for the county to contribute to the North Carolina total.

Four thousand eighty-eight North Carolinians died in service. Because the State had 2.66 percent of the population of the United States, it lost more than its share–more than 3%.

Of the 4,088 Carolinians killed, Rutherford County lost 149; this was more than 3.6 percent of the deaths in the State of North Carolina. A disproportionate share of the Rutherford County servicemen made the supreme sacrifice.

The average age of the Rutherford County soldier who died in service of his country during World War II was 24 years. The youngest boy was 18; the oldest man was 42.

More than 36% of those killed from Rutherford County were married. One of these married men had 4 children; another had 3. A total of 34 children in Rutherford County lost their fathers during World War II. These 149 men from Rutherford County were undeniably "real heroes," according to John Henry Bradley.

"The real heroes . . . are the guys who didn't come back," explained John Henry Bradley, who participated in the best-known flag raising on Iwo Jima during World War II. (Bradley, p. 4) Rutherford County produced more than its share of "real heroes" during World War II.

Some people might argue that there were heroes who came back. This book does not take from them and their accomplishments but will focus only on those who did not return. The title *Real Heroes: Rutherford County Men Who Made the Supreme Sacrifice During World War II* acknowledges the importance of the gift of these 149 men to Rutherford County, to North Carolina, to the country, and to the world.

The "real heroes" from Rutherford County began their sacrifice on the day of the Japanese attack and continued their dedicated service throughout the last year of the war–1945. The first casualty from Rutherford County was at Pearl Harbor on December 7, 1941.

Mark Alexander Rhodes, Seaman, U.S. Navy, of the Providence Community, Forest City, Route 1, was Rutherford County's first casualty. Seaman Rhodes was killed in action when the ill-fated *U.S.S. Arizona* was sunk at Pearl Harbor in the treacherous attack on Sunday morning, December 7, 1941. *(Forest City Courier, August 12, 1945)*

Throughout World War II–and after–the Rutherford County military continued to give their best. World War II ended in 1945 when Germany surrendered on May 8 and when Japan capitulated on August 14.

Rutherford County's enlisted men who died in the service of their country continued throughout the year of 1945, however. Although World War II was over in August, Rutherford County men in the military had to complete tours of duty and endure continued exposure to illness and to danger. Four additional men from Rutherford County died in military service after August 14 but before the end of 1945. The total servicemen who died between December 7, 1941, and December 31, 1945, from Rutherford County reached 149.

Those at home in Rutherford County had to endure hardships also.

Scarcely a home in Rutherford County but was affected in some manner by the selective service. The sentiment was almost unanimous that the war must be won. Those at home were deter-mined to do their part and bring the boys back home at the earliest practical moment. Women entered industry to take the place of men who had gone to war. A manpower shortage developed, which required not only the women, but also the older folk, in retirement, to again enter the list of workers. All of Rutherford County's textile plants were producing war goods, and operating on full schedule. This called for many additional workers. Then President Roosevelt appealed to the American people saying that America must be the arsenal of democracy.

The manpower shortage was keenly felt on the farms. The farmers were called upon to increase both their acreage and production per acre. This they managed to do, in face of the fact that increased production was attained with less help than in the days when production was much lower.

With about one-fourth of the country's available manpower in service, the citizens at home had to shoulder the additional load and double production, in mills, on farms, with two men instead of eight.

But long hours of production was not the entire story. Many of these workers were connected with the various branches of the Office of Civilian Defense, which took up what little leisure time they had. (Griffin, p. 19)

What was the attitude of those remaining in Rutherford County? Rutherford County mothers and fathers never forgot the child who was away; wives continued to grieve absent husbands; children missed their fathers.

Religious faith helped many at home–and abroad–to endure. Most churches in Rutherford County were open for daily prayer. A news story in *The Rutherford County News* reminded the public of this fact.

The churches of the town are open for any who care to come into the beauty and holiness of a sacred place for minutes of prayer and meditation. "And I set my face unto the Lord God, to seek by prayer and supplication." (*Rutherford County News*, May 11, 1944)

The ringing of the church bells at noon each day is the call to prayer . . . Any and all citizens are urged to share in these seasons of prayer. At that time one of the churches is open for any who will deny themselves a few minutes to come and join in the privileges of prayer. Any and all citizens are urged to share in these seasons of united prayer for our churches, our nation, our world, our fellow-citizens in the armed forces, and the coming of the King of Peace. If you care, come to the church for prayer. But wherever you are, take a few minutes immediately following the ringing of the bells for earnest, fervent prayer. (*Rutherford County News,* May 11, 1944)

The servicemen from Rutherford County entered all branches of service: the U.S. Army, the U.S. Marines, the U.S. Navy, and the U.S. Army Air Forces. They served as Paratroopers, Fighter Pilots, Tail Gunners, Waist Gunners, Medics, Infantrymen, Seamen, and Engineers–to name a few of their roles. The performed their appointed tasks–big and small–as they had been taught to do: to the best of their ability.

Back home, blue stars hung in the windows to mark the absence of a family member in service. Many of these stars changed to gold as telegrams and letters arrived announcing the loss of the loved one.

Three Rutherford County families received two such notices; the Ruppe, McKinney, and Hall families sadly but proudly changed two blue stars in their windows to gold ones. Their six "real heroes" were Lynn T. (September 23, 1943) and Toy Ruppe (September 13, 1944); Daniel K. (January 25, 1945) and Gilkey A. Hall, Jr. (June 7, 1944); and Broadus H. (December 11, 1944) and R. Earl McKinney (September 22, 1944).

Tri-High School sacrificed also. Seventeen young men from Tri-High School–which served Avondale, Henrietta, and Caroleen–died in the service of their country.

The former Tri-High School.
Now known as the Thomas Jefferson Charter School.

A marker to their memory is at the original site of that school, now the Thomas Jefferson Charter School on Highway 221-A and near Cliffside. The ones who died were "Herman Cicero Adkins, Jack Allen,

William Alexander Bailey, Charles Eugene Ballard, James Thomas Green, James Wilbur Harrill, Vernon Joseph Lowery, Daniel Dewitt Mason, Frank Browning Morehead, Joseph Madison Price, Roy Robertson, Carl Jacob Schwartz, Baxter Wiseman Tate, R. O. Tessnear, Robert Ward, Ralph Walden Waycaster, and Darrel Justice Wilson."

Memorial marker at Tri-High School.

The "real heroes" from Rutherford County distinguished themselves. Not only did they respond to the challenge, they excelled in their service to their country. Those in command bestowed upon the Rutherford County "real heroes" many awards; some of these awards were posthumous. Their numerous awards and decorations included the Bronze Star, the Oak-Leaf Cluster, the Silver Star, the Air Medal, the Good Conduct Medal, the Expert, and the Sharpshooter Medal. One Rutherford County man received the Soldier's Medal, an award given primarily to an Armed Forces member who demonstrated heroism not involving actual conflict with an enemy; the performance must have involved personal hazard or danger and the voluntary risk of life under conditions not involving conflict with an armed enemy. (http://www.usarotc.com/medals/sm.htm) Each of the "real heroes" from Rutherford County received the Purple Heart. From 1932 until September of 1942, this award was for merit and for war wounds; thereafter, the award went only to those classified as KIA (killed in action), WIA (wounded in action), or DOW (died of wounds).

These many awards were fitting, deserved, and appreciated; but we, too, can bestow upon them an important gift: we can remember. The purpose of *Real Heroes* is to make sure that Rutherford County remembers those who did not return; their faces and facts are fast fading. Please supply me with any updates and photographs needed for a future edition.

Most citizens did not realize that the Army Chaplain Corps suffered a higher percentage of casualties than any group other than the U.S. Army Air Forces and the Infantry. Yards from the Normandy front, this chaplain is conducting a July 4, 1944, service.

ADKINS, HERMAN CICERO
September 17, 1943

Mrs. Ruby E. Adkins of near Forest City received word from the War Department that her husband, Private First Class Herman Cicero Adkins, 28, was killed in action September 17, 1943, in North Africa. He was the son of Noah Adkins, Henrietta. He entered the U.S. Army on August 10, 1942. He married Ruby Morrow on September 21, 1941. Private First Class Adkins (March 2, 1915-September 17, 1943) was a former employee of the Alexandria Mills and attended Tri-High School where he was a popular student. Private First Class Adkins made a total of 24 young men from Rutherford County who had lost their lives in World War Two. (*Rutherford County News*, October 21, 1943) He is buried in the High Shoal Baptist Cemetery. (http://rfci.net/wdfloyd/)

ALLEN, JACK
July 27, 1944

Private Jack Allen, aged 19, son of Deputy Sheriff and Mrs. Jess Allen of Caroleen, was killed in action in France, July 27. His wife, Mrs. Mary Ann Gamble Allen, and small son reside in Forest City.

Private Jack Allen entered the U.S. Army on October 8, 1943, and went overseas in March of this year. He was 19 years of age on July 14.

His parents; his wife; a four-month-old son, Jesse L. Allen; and one brother, Albert Allen of Charlotte, survived him. Private Allen (July 14, 1925-July 27, 1944) was a student at Tri-High School when he entered the U.S. Army last October. (*Forest City Courier*, August 24, 1944) He is buried in the Avondale Cemetery.
(http://rfci.net/wdfloyd/)

*Photo courtesy of
Margaret Allen*

AUTRY, HERMAN M.
July 1944

Private Frank Autry, U.S. Army, of the Shiloh Community, Rutherfordton, Route 1, was killed in France according to word received by his wife, Mrs. Elsie Cartee Autry. Private Autry was born in 1916 and was 28 at the time of his death. (*Forest City Courier*, August 10, 1944)

BACH, ROBERT ARNOLD
February 25, 1945

Technical Sergeant Robert Bach (1915-1945) was killed in action in Germany on February 25, 1945, according to a message from the War Department received Tuesday by his wife, Mrs. Elizabeth Lawing Bach, of West End, Forest City.

While attending Sunday church services, Mrs. Bach received the message notifying her that her husband, a member of an Infantry Regiment, was missing in action in Germany, since February 25th.

Sergeant Bach had entered the U.S. Army four years before and had been overseas four months. He was born on November 30, 1918, in Fairbury, Illinois.

He was a son of Mr. and Mrs. J. N. Bach of Fairbury, Illinois. He was survived by his parents, six brothers, and three sisters; his wife, Mrs. Elizabeth Lawing Bach, daughter of Mr. and Mrs. S. L. Lawing of West End, Forest City; two children, Suzanne and Tommy Bach. (*Forest City Courier*, March 29, 1945)

Photo courtesy of
Mrs. Elizabeth Bach Morris

BAILEY, WILLIAM ALEXANDER
April 13, 1945

Sergeant William Alexander Bailey, 25, son of Mr. and Mrs. Bob Bailey of Avondale, was killed in action in Germany on April 13, 1945, according to a message received by his wife, Mrs. Eunice Robertson Bailey of West End, Forest City. He was a member of a U.S. Army Field Artillery Unit.

His wife; one daughter, two-years-old; his parents; one sister; and a brother, who was also in service and was in Germany, survived young Bailey. (*Forest City Courier*, May 3, 1945)

Memorial services for Sergeant William A. Bailey (September 24, 1917-April 13, 1945), Forest City, Route 2, who died of wounds received in action, were held at Adaville Church, Oakland Community, Sunday at 2:30 o'clock.

Sergeant Bailey entered the U.S. Army March 27, 1941, and was a member of the 44th Field Artillery. He went overseas in January of 1944 and died April 13, 1945, of wounds received in action in Germany.

The memorial address was by the Reverend R. L. Crawford. The Reverend Olen Kendrick read the scripture and led the opening prayer. The presentation of the flag and medal was by Major J. J. Tarlton, Commander of the Second Battalion of the North Carolina State Guard. D. C. Cole blew taps, and the Reverend J. B. Tabor pronounced the benediction. (*Rutherford County News*, October 11, 1945)

At the request of his next of kin, R. C. Bailey, Box 190, Avondale, Sergeant William A. Bailey was brought to the United States aboard the United States Army Transport *Haiti Victory* in 1949. The remains of 91 North Carolinians who lost their lives during World War II were returned at that time. The armed forces dead originally interred in temporary military cemeteries in Northern France, Holland, and Luxembourg were among those returned in 1949. (*Forest City Courier*, March 18, 1949) He is buried in the Adaville Baptist Church Cemetery. (http://rfci.net/wdfloyd/)

BALLARD, CHARLES EUGENE
October 6, 1944

Private Charles Eugene Ballard (1925-1944) of Caroleen was killed in action in Italy on October 6, according to a telegram from the War Department. His parents, Mr. and Mrs. Henry Ballard of Caroleen, received the message Friday.

Private Ballard, U.S. Army, enlisted in the Coast Artillery in January of 1942 and had been overseas about 15 months.

He was survived by his parents; two sisters: Louise and Gwendolyn Ballard, at home; three brothers: Private First Class Glenn Ballard who was seriously wounded in action six weeks before and was with the U.S. Army in England; Private First Class Earl Ballard, U.S. Army Air Corps, stationed in France; and David Ballard, at home. (*Forest City Courier*, October 26, 1944)

BARNES, JAMES M.
April 9, 1945

Private James M. Barnes, aged 36, son of Mr. and Mrs. G. B. Barnes of near Rutherfordton, was killed in action in Germany April 9th, according to a wire from the War Department. Private Barnes (1908-1945) entered the U.S. Army on March 15, 1943, and went overseas last October. Southern Bell Telephone Company employed him before he entered service. (*Forest City Courier*, May 3, 1945)

BARRINS, CARL L.
April 6, 1945

Private Carl L. Barrins of Ellenboro, Route 1, was killed in action in Germany on April 6, 1945. The War Department this week informed his sister, Mrs. Maggie Hunt of Ellenboro, Route 1, of Carl's death. Private Barrins (May 5, 1915-April 6, 1945) was a member of a U.S. Army Infantry Unit. (*Rutherford County News*, April 26, 1945) He is buried in the Brook's Chapel Methodist Church Cemetery. (http://rfci.net/wdfloyd/)

BASS, EVERETT LEE
October 1, 1943

World War II took another victim in the death of Everett Lee Bass, 26, son of the Reverend and Mrs. R. L. Bass of Spindale. Sergeant Bass was killed Saturday while flying a U.S. Army Air Forces plane on a test flight over the Gulf of Mexico three miles from Cameron, Louisiana. There was no possibility of recovering his body.

Sergeant Bass (1917-1943) enlisted in the U.S. Army Air Forces on May 13, 1942, and received training at Keesler Field, Biloxi, Mississippi; at Roosevelt Field, New York; and at the Curtis-Wright Airfield, Buffalo, New York. At the time of his death he was a tail gunner on a bomber and was located at Lake Charles, Louisiana.

The telegram received by his parents stated: "We deeply regret to inform you of the death of your son, Everett, in an aircraft accident near Cameron, Louisiana, in the Gulf of New Mexico, October 1. Mrs. Louis Bass, wife of the deceased, was here at Lake Charles, Louisiana, and had been notified. Richard D. Dick, Lieutenant Colonel, U.S. Army Air Corps."

Sergeant Bass was a member of the Spindale Methodist Church, of which his father was pastor.

Besides his parents he was survived by his wife; one young brother, Billy; three sisters: Mary Lou Bass of Charlotte; Mrs. H. A. Allred of Pompano, California; and Sarah Bass of Spindale; and his grandmother, Mrs. Bell Wood of Vale.

Sergeant Bass was married about two weeks ago, but the wedding had not been made public. (*Rutherford County News*, October 7, 1943)

BEARDEN, RANDALL B.

First Lieutenant Randall B. Bearden from Rutherford County, North Carolina, lost his life in World War II. He was in the U.S. Army. No other information is available.

BLANTON, THOMAS H.
February 3, 1942

Private First Class Thomas H. Blanton died in a base hospital at Fort Benning, Georgia, Tuesday morning of an accidentally inflicted bullet wound. Private Blanton, a son of Mr. and Mrs. Clarence Blanton of Cliffside, was a member of Battery "B," 14th Field Artillery of the Second Army Division.

According to reports, Private Blanton and another soldier, who had been on guard duty, entered their quarters Monday night and prepared to holster their pistols. The gun in the hand of Blanton's comrade was in some manner accidentally discharged, the bullet striking Private First Class Blanton (March 29, 1922-February 3, 1942). He was taken to the U.S. Army hospital where he died Tuesday morning.

The body will arrive at Cliffside (via Southern Railway according to the *Rutherford County News*, February 5, 1942) about noon Thursday (today). Funeral services will be held Friday afternoon at three o'clock at the Cliffside Baptist Church, of which he was a member, and interment will be in the Cliffside Cemetery. His parents, Mr. and Mrs. Clarence Blanton of Cliffside, and six brothers survived him. (Spindale Sun, February 5, 1942)

Blanton was the first to be buried in the County as a result of the Second World War. (*Rutherford County News*, February 5, 1946) He is buried in the Cliffside Cemetery. (http://rfci.net/wdfloyd/)

BOST, ROBERT W.
June 13, 1944

Sergeant Robert Bost, U.S. Army Air Corps, was reported missing in action over Germany on June 12, 1944. He was a gunner on a bomber. He was a son of Mrs. J. W. Bost and the late Mr. Bost. This message from the War Department came to his wife who lived with her parents near town. (*Rutherfordton County News*, June 28, 1944)

Sergeant Robert Bost (December 26, 1920-June 13, 1944) of Spindale, son of Mrs. J. W. Bost and the late Mr. Bost, reported missing in action since June 13, 1944, was presumed to be dead, according to a War Department letter received by his wife.

> The record concerning your husband shows that he was a crew member of a B-24 Liberator airplane that collided with another plane in mid-air; both aircraft were seen to break apart and fall earthward, while returning from a bombing mission in Munich, Germany.

> Full consideration has recently been given to all available information bearing on the absence of your husband, and considered in view of the fact that 12 months have expired without receipt of evidence to support a continued presumption of survival, the War Department must terminate such absence by a presumptive finding of death.

Sergeant Bost was graduated from Rutherfordton-Spindale Central High School in the Class of 1939. Before entering service in March 1943, he was employed by Dan River Cotton Mills, Danville, Virginia. He took training at Keesler Field, Mississippi; gunnery school at Laredo, Texas; and at the U.S. Army air base at Salt Lake City, Utah; Biggs Field, El Paso, Texas; and Topeka, Kansas.

He was survived by his mother, Mrs. J. W. Bost; his wife, the former Miss Melba Hoyle; their two-year-old daughter, Diane; two sisters: Madge Bost and Mrs. Charlie Schuler of Spindale; one brother, Howard, who spent nine months overseas and had recently received a discharge from the U.S. Army.

Sergeant Bost's death brought Rutherford County's World War II total dead to 116 men, with 19 still reported missing. (*Forest City Courier*, June 28, 1945) He is buried in the Spindale Cemetery. (http://rfci.net/wdfloyd/)

BRACKETT, JOHN O.
December 12, 1945

Private First Class John O. Brackett, aged 34, was burned to death on December 12, 1945, at Hanshua, Japan, according to a message from the Chaplain received Friday by the family. According to the brief details, a large two-story frame building, in which his company was bivouacked, burned during the early morning hours. All men escaped except Brackett and another soldier. Their bodies, when discovered in the ashes next morning, indicated that Private First Class Brackett had made an attempt to save his comrade. He was buried in the U.S. Army Cemetery at Eta Jima No. 1, a small island near Kure, Japan.

Private First Class Brackett (1911-1945) entered service on January 24, 1945, and went overseas August 5, 1945. He was survived by his wife, the former Selma Propes of Belwood; his parents, Mr. and Mrs. D. O. Brackett of Forest City; six sisters, Mrs. Worth Houser, Rutherfordton; Mrs. H. P. Harrill and Mrs. Graham Wall, Forest City; Mrs. Ray Tranthem, Charlotte; Mrs. Hubert Harrill, Blue Ridge, Georgia; and Miss Bobbie Brackett at home.

The family had not yet received official notice of his death from the War Department when this article was published. (*Forest City Courier*, January 24, 1946)

Mrs. John O. Brackett of Forest City received the posthumously awarded Soldier's Medal for her husband's heroism in Japan at Moore General Hospital in Swannanoa, North Carolina, on April 10, 1946.

Lieutenant Colonel Fred Brillinger presented the award in the presence of Private Brackett's mother, Mrs. D. O. Brackett, and his sister and her husband, Mr. and Mrs. H. P. Harrill.

31

The citation reads:

For heroism at Zentsuji, Shiloku, Japan, on December 7, 1945. At approximately 0330 a fire broke out in one of company's barracks at Zentsuji, Shiloku, Japan. Private Brackett was the first one in his room to awaken. After awakening the rest of the occupants in the room, he left the room to aid the other men in the building. He would have escaped the fire if he had not stayed to help others in the building. Private Brackett's utter disregard for his own personal safety, his coolness and presence of mind undoubtedly save the lives of many of his comrades, and reflect the utmost credit upon himself and the military service. (*Forest City Courier*, April 18, 1946)

Photo courtesy of Daily Courier, Forest City, North Carolina, and James R. Brown, Publisher

BRANCH, THOMAS O.
December 9, 1944

Private Thomas O. Branch, son of Mr. and Mrs. George O. Branch of Rutherfordton, Route 2, died December 9, 1944, of wounds received in action.

He entered the U.S. Army on December 14, 1943, went overseas August 14, 1944, and was serving with the Infantry of the 35th Division.

His wife, Blanche Shehan Branch, of Rutherfordton, Route 2; a daughter, Shirley Ann; his parents; one brother, Troy Branch of the U.S. Navy; and six sisters survived him.

The Bronze Star was post-humously awarded to his wife for his gallantry in action. He was wounded while removing other wounded men from the front lines in Germany and later died of his wounds. (*Forest City Courier*, September 13, 1945)

The Bronze Star was awarded posthumously to Private Thomas O. Branch (1918-1944) for gallantry in action in Germany. While removing wounded in November of 1944, he was wounded himself and later died of his wounds.

Members of the family were special guests of the Lions Club. Mrs. Branch received the award on behalf of her husband.

O. J. Mooneyham made a short address in which he cited Rutherford County's part in World War II, both on the home front and on the battle-field. He then presented Colonel Fox who formally awarded the medal and read the official War Department citation.

Captain Thomas A. Roberts, himself the holder of two high U.S. Army awards, was recognized as a special guest of the club. Miss Bobby Brackett sang "God Bless America," accompanied by Miss Virginia McDowell. (*Forest City Courier*, September 6, 1945)

Photo courtesy of <u>Daily Courier</u>, Forest City, North Carolina, and James R. Brown, Publisher

BRIDGES, D. S. BOYCE, JR.
March 23, 1945

D. S. Boyce Bridges, Jr., was born June 20, 1924, in a house next to the school on Main Street in Cliffside, North Carolina. He was the youngest of seven children of Doctor Samuel Boyce Bridges, Sr., and Retter Daves Bridges. Boyce, Jr., attended school in Cliffside and was graduated from Cliffside High School in 1940. During his boyhood he was a member of the Cliffside Boy Scout Troop No. 1, and he joined Cliffside Baptist Church when he was eight years old. He attended Clemson College and on December 25, 1941, he married Mary Elizabeth Carpenter.

On November 20, 1942, Boyce, Jr., enlisted in the U.S. Army Air Corps and began training in Miami Beach, Florida. During his cadet training period, he was stationed at Lebanon and Nashville, Tennessee; Maxwell Field, Alabama; and Jackson and Greenville, Mississippi. Boyce, Jr., received his pilot's wings and was commissioned as a Second Lieutenant at Jackson Army Air Base in Mississippi on April 15, 1944. He was sent overseas on September 18, 1944, and served in the 406th Fighter Squadron, 371st Fighter Group in the European Theater of Operations. Because his first given name was Doctor, his fellow servicemen called him "Doc."

As a P-47 Thunderbolt Fighter Pilot, Lieutenant Bridges flew 58 missions from England to the continent during the last days of World War II. For his outstanding service, he was promoted to the rank of First Lieutenant on March 20, 1945. On March 23, 1945, he successfully dive-bombed a ferry on the Rhine. In the face of intense anti-aircraft fire, he gallantly descended to minimum altitude to strafe an enemy transport and gun position near Speyer, Germany. His plane was caught in enemy flak and crashed. Lieutenant Bridges escaped from the plane but was shot and killed by a sniper. His body was found by the Allies one hour later as they took the town.

Lieutenant Bridges was initially interred in the St. Avold American Military Cemetery in France. In 1948 his remains were sent home to rest in the Cliffside Cemetery. His monument is the tallest one in that cemetery.

Lieutenant Boyce Bridges, Jr., posthumously received the following awards and decorations: the Silver Star Medal, the Air Medal with Four Oak-Leaf Clusters, the Purple Heart for having made the supreme sacrifice in the service of his country, the European-African Middle Eastern Theater Ribbon with two Bronze Service Stars for the Rhineland and

Central Europe Campaigns, the World War II Victory Ribbon, the Pilot Aviation Badge, the American Theater Ribbon, and the Good Conduct Medal. His name is engraved on the Greenville County (SC) Veterans Wall of Remembrance and the Battle of Normandy Foundation Wall of Liberty. He is an honoree of the World War II Memorial to be completed by 2004 in Washington, D.C. *(Submitted by nieces Anne C. Cargill and Paula M. Cargill and by nephew John B. Cargill)*

Photo Courtesy of Nieces Anne C. Cargill and Paula M. Cargill and nephew John B. Cargill.

Bridges, D. S. Boyce, Jr., with his Mother, Retter Daves Bridges, after he was commissioned Second Lieutenant on April 15, 1944, in Cliffside, North Carolina

Photo Courtesy of Nieces Anne C. Cargill and Paula M. Cargill and Nephew John B. Cargill

Major (Later Lieutenant Colonel) Paul Bridges and his brother Bridges, D. S. Boyce, Jr. – March 23, 1945

Photo courtesy of Nieces Anne C. Cargill and Paula M. Cargill and Nephew John B. Cargill

BRIDGES, D. S. BOYCE, JR.
March 23, 1945

Second Lieutenant Boyce Bridges, Jr., and Major H. Paul Bridges of Cliffside met in France after a period of two years without having seen each other. The two brothers were stationed in French towns only a few miles apart. Second Lieutenant Bridges was a pilot in the U.S. Army Air Corps, and Major Bridges was with the Quartermaster Corps. Major Bridges saw his brother in uniform for the first time; neither have ever had leaves at the same time since they have been in service. They were the only sons of Mrs. Boyce Bridges and the late Mr. Bridges of Cliffside. First Lieutenant Bridges's wife was the former Miss Mary Carpenter of Avondale, and Major Bridges's wife was the former Miss Hazel Haynes of Cliffside. (*Forest City Courier,* January 25, 1945)

First Lieutenant D. S. Boyce Bridges, Jr., of Cliffside, was killed March 23, in Germany, according to a War Department message received by his wife. First Lieutenant Bridges (June 20, 1924*-March 23, 1945) entered service from Clemson College in February 1943. He received his commission as Second Lieutenant in the Air Corps at Jackson, Mississippi, on April 5, 1944. He left for overseas duty on September 18, 1944. First Lieutenant Bridges was a P-47 Thunderbolt pilot with the Ninth Air Force. He had completed 56 missions and had received the Air Medal and Four Oak-Leaf Clusters. He was promoted to First Lieutenant three days before his death.

First Lieutenant Bridges's brother, Major H. Paul Bridges, was stationed only a few miles from his brother's air base in France; they spent several hours together only two days before First Lieutenant Bridges's death. Major Bridges was able to obtain many details concerning First Lieutenant Bridges's death and to write about them to his family. First Lieutenant Bridges was to be buried with military honors and ceremonies by his group. At the time Major Bridges wrote, the services had not been held, and he was to be notified of the time and place so that he could attend.

First Lieutenant Bridges was survived by his wife, Mrs. Mary Carpenter Bridges of Avondale; his mother, Mrs. Boyce Bridges, Sr., of Cliffside; three sisters: Mrs. Mabel Cargill of Henrietta, Mrs. Inez Ashe of Greensboro, and Miss Wytle Bridges of Cliffside; and one brother, Major H. Paul Bridges, in France. (*Forest City Courier*, April 12, 1945)

*The marker at the cemetery is in error. Although Boyce Bridges was actually born on June 20, 1924, his marker at the Cliffside Cemetery has June 24, 1924, as his birth date.

Memorial services for First Lieutenant D. S. Boyce Bridges were held at Temple Baptist Church at Henrietta, Sunday afternoon, April 22. Ministers taking part in the services were the Reverend F. E. Dabney, pastor of the Temple Church; the Reverend J. A. Hunnicutt of Greenville, South Carolina; the Reverend O. D. Moore of Cliffside; and Chaplain L. W. Cain, who had recently returned from service overseas. There was special music by the choir, and Miss Virginia Christy of Avondale sang, "Crossing the Bar" with Miss Lucile Wall at the piano. Mr. Hunnicutt paid high tribute to Lieutenant Bridges as a young man of admirable qualities and sterling character. He was beloved by everyone and had scores of friends who mourn his untimely death. Chaplain Cain in his remarks paid high tribute to young men of America who were making the supreme sacrifice in the war. Having just returned from long months overseas with men in combat service, he was qualified to know what our soldiers were going through and the unselfish sacrifices they were making.

The high esteem in which First Lieutenant Bridges was held was evidenced by the numbers of friends attending the service; many of them stood throughout the service. There were many beautiful flowers as a farewell tribute.

First Lieutenant Bridges enlisted in the U.S. Army Air Corps in 1942 while he was a student at Clemson. He went overseas in September of 1944 and served in the European theatre of operations. He was a pilot of the P-47 Thunderbolt fighter plane and was promoted to First Lieutenant only three days before his death. He was killed on March 23 over Germany. (*Forest City Courier*, May 3, 1945)

The Silver Star was awarded posthumously to First Lieutenant Boyce Bridges, Jr., Cliffside, "for gallantry in action while participating in aerial flight against the enemy on 23 March 1945." First Lieutenant Bridges was killed over Germany on March 23. He was a pilot of a P-47 Thunderbolt plane.

The medal will be presented to his wife, Mrs. Mary Carpenter Bridges of Henrietta, at a later date. (*Forest City Courier*, August 16, 1945)

In a ceremony at her home Sunday afternoon at 3 o'clock, Mrs. Boyce Bridges, Jr., of Henrietta, received the Silver Star Medal and Air Medal with two Oak Leaf Clusters awarded posthumously to her husband, First Lieutenant Boyce Bridges, Jr. Colonel Wilbur J. Fox of Camp Croft, South Carolina, made the awards. The invocation and benediction were by the Reverend L. W. Cain of the Temple Baptist Church of Henrietta.

The citations for the medals are as follow:

Air Medal and Two Oak-Leaf Clusters: "For meritorious Air achievement while participating in sustained operational flights against the enemy."

Silver Star:

For gallantry in action while participating in aerial flight against the enemy on March 23, 1945. Lieutenant Bridges exhibited extraordinary courage and devotion to duty while leading a flight on a bombing mission in conjunction with air-ground operations. After successfully dive-bombing a ferry on the Rhine, in the face of intense anti-aircraft fire, he gallantly descended to minimum altitude to strike an enemy transport and gun positions. His superior airmanship and determination despite innumerable odds were contributing factors to the success of the allied air offensive and were in keeping with the highest traditions of the Army Air Forces.

First Lieutenant Bridges was killed March 23 while on a flight over Germany. His wife was the former Miss Mary Carpenter of Henrietta. He was the son of Mrs. Boyce Bridges and the late Mr. Boyce Bridges. (*Rutherford County News*, January 10, 1946) He is buried in the Cliffside Cemetery. (http://rfci.net/wdfloyd/)

BRIDGES, IVEN E.
December 14, 1944

Private First Class Iven E. Bridges of Ellenboro was killed in action on Leyte, December 14, 1944, according to a message received by his mother, Mrs. James D. Bridges of Ellenboro. He was 22 years of age last July.

A member of the Infantry Anti-Tank corps, Private First Class Bridges (July 24, 1922-December 14, 1944) entered the U.S. Army on December 27, 1942, and was trained at Fort McClellan, Alabama, and in a camp in California.

After his training, he went to Australia in April of 1943.

He was survived by his mother; three sisters: Mrs. C. S. Clayton, Mrs. Paul Helms of Charlotte, and Mrs. H. C. McGinnis of Rutherfordton; four brothers: T. O. Bridges of Charlotte; Glenn Bridges of Ellenboro; Oris Bridges of Spindale; and Sergeant Hal Bridges, now in Germany. (*Forest City Courier*, January 25, 1945) He is buried in the Bethel Baptist Church Cemetery. (http://rfci.net/wdfloyd/)

Private First Class Bridges was a resident of Charlotte and employed in Charlotte when inducted into the Army at Fort Jackson, South Carolina, December 27, 1942. He took his basic training at Fort McClellan, Alabama, from January of 1943 until March of 1943. He went overseas to Australia for advanced training and was in action in New Guinea and the Philippines. He was killed on Leyte Island on December 14, 1944. *(Information from Charles and Judy Bridges)*

Photo courtesy of Charles and Judy Bridges

BRIGHT, LEROY
January 3, 1945

Staff Sergeant Leroy Bright, aged 22, was killed in action in Belgium January 3, 1945, according to a message received by his wife, the former Miss Lillian Fleming of Bogalusa, Louisiana. He was a son of Mr. and Mrs. C. H. Bright of Forest City, Route 2.

Staff Sergeant Bright (December 16, 1922-January 3, 1945) entered service in June of 1940 and served in South America three years. He was next stationed at Camp Shelby, Mississippi, where he received training as a Paratrooper. He went overseas November 1, 1944.

He was survived by his wife, the former Miss Lillian Fleming of Bogalusa, Louisiana; parents; three brothers: Corporal Vannoy Bright, who was serving in Germany; Walter and Junior Bright, at home; three sisters, Mrs. Earl Haulk of Forest City, and Mavis and Joan Bright at home. (*Forest City Courier*, January 25, 1942)

The letter from Chaplain Kenneth N. Engle to Sergeant Bright's mother stated in part:

> [Sergeant Bright's] contribution to the freedom and peace of the world was far beyond anything that words can express. He became known as an outstanding platoon sergeant in this campaign. He was killed during his unit's heroic stand against the recent desperate breakthrough of the German's at Bastogne. He and his comrades' stubborn defense of this sector is believed to be responsible for the stopping of the enemy's all-out drive. I realize that this is little consolation for your loss but we know that the future generations of the world will be given a better life because he and others fought so grandly to control the German threat. I feel that he has no regrets. As a parachutist he was always willing to take more than his share of the hardships and dangers.

He is buried in an American Cemetery in Belgium near where his comrades are carrying on the struggle. The military service at the cemetery was simple but impressive. After the religious ceremony the guard of honor stood at attention while a rifle squad fired a volley of three shots over his grave. A bugle played taps and far away faintly came the echo of another bugle. He lies at rest among his comrades. A simple white cross marks his grave with the American flag flying over the cemetery. (Information furnished by Eula Mavis Bridges)

Sergeant Bright was buried in the Pleasant Grove Methodist Cemetery in May of 1949. (http://rfci.net/wdfloyd/ and Eula Mavis Bridges)

Photo on previous page courtesy of Mavis Bright Bridges

Photos courtesy of Daily Courier, Forest City, North Carolina, and James R. Brown, Publisher

BUCKNER, NORMAN HENRY
July 22, 1944

Mr. and Mrs. P. S. Buckner of West Asheville, formerly of Spindale, received a wire from Washington last week that their son Norman Henry Buckner (June 27, 1924-July 22, 1944) was killed in France on July 22, 1944. He had been in France two weeks and overseas two months. He had been in service a year. He was a member of Adaville Baptist Church, Oakland Section. (*Rutherford County News*, August 17, 1944) He is buried in the Adaville Baptist Church Cemetery. (http://rfci.net/wdfloyd/)

BURTON, MALCOLM J.
December 16, 1944

Staff Sergeant Malcolm J. Burton was wounded in action in France, July 4, according to a message received by his wife, the former Margaret Johnson of Spindale. Private First Class Burton, a native of Landrum, South Carolina, had resided in Spindale for the past nine years; he was an employee of the Sterling Hosiery Mills. His wife received the Purple Heart Medal awarded him this week. (*Forest City Courier*, July 20, 1944)

Word of the death of Staff Sergeant Malcolm J. Burton on December 16, 1944, was received in Spindale by his wife Friday. Sergeant Burton, wounded in action on December 5th, died in France as a result of those wounds.

A native of Landrum, South Carolina, Staff Sergeant Burton (1915-1944) made his home in Spindale for a number of years prior to entering the U.S. Army in 1943; he was at that time associated with the Sterling Hosiery Mills. He had been overseas approximately ten months and had been wounded once before. (*Forest City Courier*, January 11, 1945)

BYERS, JOSEPH
February 13, 1943

Father Had Three Sons in Service

First, Joe Byers (left) who was transferred from Fort Eustis, Virginia, to the Panama Canal Zone. Center, S. K. Byers of Rutherfordton, father of three sons in the service. Right, Mosee Byers, 6th Battery, 605th Anti-Aircraft Artillery, Camp Stewart, Georgia.

A third son of Mrs. and Mrs. Byers, Private Roy Byers, ASN 1008917 Company "A", 392nd Quartermaster Battalion, (Port) A P 0 810 Iceland, was not in the picture. He had been in Iceland a year. His parents had heard nothing from him within two months. He wrote his mother here once a week for three years while he was in a Civilian Conservation Corps camp.

All three boys liked the U.S. Army. They were doing their part to help with the war. (*Rutherfordton County News*, May 14, 1942)

Mr. and Mrs. S. K. Byers of Rutherfordton were notified in March of the accidental drowning of their son Private Joseph Byers (1925-1943) of the U.S. Army. He was drowned in Puerto Rico on February 13, 1943. (*Forest City Courier*, December 16, 1943)

Photos courtesy of Daily Courier, Forest City, North Carolina, and James R. Brown, Publisher

CARTEE, ZEB C.
June 6, 1944

Private Zeb Cartee, son of Mr. and Mrs. B. L. Cartee of Rutherfordton, Route 1, Shiloh Community, was missing since June 6 in France. He was a member of an engineering unit. He entered service February 22, 1942, and had been overseas one year. His parents received the message Friday that he was missing. He was a brother of Hollis Cartee, who was in an anti-aircraft unit in North Africa. (*Forest City Courier*, July 13, 1944)

Private Zeb C. Cartee, 24, member of an Engineer unit, previously reported missing in action on June 6, 1944, was reported killed in action in France, according to a War Department message, received by his parents, Mr. and Mrs. B. L. Cartee of Rutherfordton, Route 1, residents of the Shiloh community.

Private Cartee volunteered for the U.S. Army on February 21, 1941, and had been overseas for 15 months. He was a member of Corinth Baptist Church, near Ellenboro, at the time of his death.

Private Cartee (April 18,1920-June 6, 1944) was survived by his parents, Mr. and Mrs. B. L. Cartee, and the following brothers and sisters: Jessie L. Cartee, Baltimore, Maryland; Mrs. Elsie Radford, Evelyn, Ralph, Troy, Ida, Audry at home; Mrs. Lillian Hawkins, Forest City; and Private Hollis D. Cartee in North Africa. (*Forest City Courier*, September 7, 1944) He is buried in the Prospect Baptist Cemetery, Spartanburg, County. (http://rfci.net/wdfloyd/)

CHAPMAN, ALBERT C.
February 25, 1945

Staff Sergeant Albert Chapman (1924-1945) of Rutherfordton was killed in action in Germany on February 25, according to an announcement from the War Department to his parents, Mr. and Mrs. W. M. Chapman.

A wire reported Staff Sergeant Chapman of the U.S. Army was missing in action; a second wire brought word that he was dead.

Staff Sergeant Chapman had been in service two years and overseas approximately one year. He had two brothers in service; they were W. A. Chapman in Belgium and Ray Chapman in Germany. (*Forest City Courier*, March 29, 1945)

COBB, RUSH
May 4, 1945

Private First Class Rush Cobb, 31, was killed in action on Luzon on May 4, 1945, according to a message received from the War Department by his wife, the former Janie Thrift of Cliffside. His death brought Rutherford County's total World War II dead to 115 men.

Private First Class Cobb, son of Mr. and Mrs. R. O. Cobb of Cliffside, entered the U.S. Army on December 27, 1942. Trained at Camp Croft, South Carolina, and Camp Butner, North Carolina, he was a member of an Infantry Regiment. He went overseas December 31, 1943, and served in Hawaii, New Guinea, and the Philippines. He was killed on Luzon.

Private First Class Cobb (1914-1945) was survived by his wife; his parents; one sister, Mary Helen Cobb, Cliffside; five brothers, Taft and Worth Cobb, at home; Corporal Ray Cobb and Private Russell Cobb, both in Germany; and Marshall Cobb, Seaman First Class, U.S. Navy, somewhere in the Pacific. (*Forest City Courier*, June 21, 1945)

Photo courtesy of Daily Courier, Forest City, North Carolina, and James R. Brown, Publisher

COCHRAN, ROBERT
March 19, 1945

Sergeant First Class Robert Cochran (1925-1945) of Union Mills was killed on March 19, 1945. Sergeant First Class Cochran was in the U.S. Navy. *(Information is courtesy of Nancy Stallcup's Memorial Garden Honor Roll.)*

COLLINS, EARNEST P.
July 6, 1944

Mr. and Mrs. Rinnie Collins of near Rutherfordton, Shiloh section, received a wire from Washington, August 2, 1944, that their son Private First Class Earnest P. Collins was killed in action July 6, 1944, in France. Private First Class Collins (1922-1944) entered the U.S. Army on March 1, 1943, and took his basic training at Little Rock, Arkansas. He was in the Infantry. He had a brother, Private Gomer H. Collins, in service in England, and a brother Thurman Collins at home. (*Forest City Courier*, February 8, 1945) In addition to his parents and two brothers, two sisters also survived; they were Mrs. O. P. Sparks of Spindale and Delma Collins of the home. Private First Class Collins had, in addition to the brother in service, a sister-in-law and 32 cousins in service of their country.

Private First Class Collins had been in service 16 months and overseas about three months. He was a member of the Baptist Church and was well-known in this section. (*Rutherford County News*, September 21, 1944)

Photo courtesy of <u>Daily Courier</u>, Forest City, North Carolina, and James R. Brown, Publisher

COMPTON, JOE FOCH
December 26, 1942

Lieutenant Joe Foch Compton was killed in action December 26, 1942, somewhere in the Southwest Pacific area. The first word received by the family in regard to his death was on January 29, 1943, when two letters addressed to him were returned marked, "Killed in Action."

Mr. and Mrs. Compton received official notice from the War Department of their son's death.

Lieutenant Compton (1919-1942) and his twin brother, Lieutenant John Pershing Compton, also of the Air Corps, were born May 8, 1918, in Spartanburg County, South Carolina. They were educated at Cliffside High School and at Boiling Springs Junior College; each had two years at Wofford College. Both took a CAA course at Wofford, and they entered the U.S. Army Air Corps in May of 1942. Lieutenant John Compton was overseas, a bombardier in the Air Corps.

Lieutenant Joe Compton was sent overseas last August. (*Rutherford County News*, February 25, 1943)

Photo courtesy of Daily Courier, Forest City, North Carolina, and James R. Brown, Publisher

*Photos courtesy of
Victoria Luckadoo*

CRAWFORD, DUDLEY W.
October 9, 1943

Ensign Dudley W. Crawford, Jr., U.S. Navy (Reserve), was reported missing in action last Thursday by the U.S. Navy Department in a wire to his mother here. Ensign Crawford entered the service in August of 1942. He was commissioned last November. He attended the University of North Carolina, Lees-McRae College, Banner Elk, and the University of California at Los Angeles; he recently taught school at Nashville, North Carolina. His father works with OPA in Washington, DC. (*Rutherford County News*, October 21, 1943)

Ensign Crawford (1920-1943) went down with the U.S.S. *Buck* (DD-420). The destroyer was sunk in the Mediterranean by a German submarine U-616 on October 9, 1943. He was survived by his parents and two sisters: Misses Mary Miller and Eloise Crawford, both of Rutherfordton.

Young Crawford entered service August 11, 1942, and was trained at Notre Dame and Northwestern Universities. He joined the fleet in January of 1943 and was commissioned in November of 1942. He was educated at Lees-McRae College, the University of North Carolina, and the University of Southern California; prior to entering the U.S. Navy, he taught school. He was 24 years of age. (*Forest City Courier*, November 2, 1944)

Ensign Dudley W. Crawford, Jr., United States Naval Reserve, was reported presumably dead after being reported missing in action since October 9, 1943. His parents, Mr. and Mrs. Dudley W. Crawford, Sr., of Rutherfordton, received a message from the Navy Department last Friday advising them that the Department had listed him as dead. (*Forest City Courier*, November 2, 1944)

CROTTS, ARNOLD B.
December 14, 1944

Private First Class Arnold B. Crotts, son of Mr. and Mrs. John Crotts of Forest City, Big Springs Avenue, was killed in action in Germany on December 14, according to a message received last week from the War Department. Private First Class Crotts (March 18, 1922-December 14, 1944) was a member of an Infantry Regiment in the U.S. Army. (*Forest City Courier*, January 4, 1945) He is buried in the Pleasant Grove Methodist Cemetery. (http://rfci.net/wdfloyd/)

DOBSON, NORWOOD HARRIS
May 8, 1944

A large crowd attended the funeral services and burial for Lieutenant (Junior Grade) U.S. Navy, Norwood Harris Dobson, 27, at Mt. Olivet Baptist Church, near Hollis, Sunday at 3 p.m. The pastor, the Reverend L. U. Jones, was in charge and was assisted by the Reverend R. L. Crawford, former pastor.

Lieutenant Dobson (February 20, 1917-May 8, 1944) married Alpha Davis, daughter of Mr. and Mrs. Will Davis of that section. He was a model young man.

Lieutenant Dobson, a U.S. Naval Pilot, was killed in a plane crash in Cape Cod Bay, Massachusetts, Monday, May 8. A graduate of Wake Forest College, he had served in the U.S. Navy three years and had won his wings and commission at Miami, Florida, in 1942.

His widow; a daughter, Edith DeShields, three weeks old; his mother, Mrs. Mary F. Dobson of Wilmington; a sister, Mrs. Edward Hansley of Wilmington; and two brothers, Thomas Dobson of the United States Army in England and Woodrow Dobson of Fayetteville, survived him. (*Rutherford County News*, May 18, 1944) He is buried in the Mt. Olivet Baptist Cemetery. (http://rfci.net/wdfloyd/)

Photo courtesy of Aylene B. Davis

GENTRY, BARNEY ALTON
June 18, 1944

Private First Class Barney Alton Gentry, 24, son of R. G. Gentry, of Forest City, died June 18th fighting in France. He entered the U.S. Army on May 22, 1942, and went overseas October 14, 1942. Private First Class Gentry (1920-1944) left his parents; a sister, Miss Guynelle Gentry, at home; and six brothers: Corporal Melvin Gentry, in Italy; Corporal Boyd Gentry, in the Aleutian Islands; Belton Gentry of Avondale; H. D., Albert, and Ike Gentry of Forest City. (*Rutherford County News*, July 27, 1944)

Photo courtesy of James F. Gentry

GILBERT, WALTER L.
May 25, 1945

Sergeant Walter L. Gilbert, son of Mr. and Mrs. J. T. Gilbert of Forest City, was declared missing since May 26 in the Pacific area. His wife, Mrs. Ruth Gilbert, also of Forest City, received the message from the chaplain of Walter's squadron.

Sergeant Gilbert (November 30, 1919-May 25, 1945) was a member of the Twentieth Air Force; he was missing in a raid over Japan. He was a waist gunner. Sergeant Gilbert entered the U.S. Army Air Forces on June 7, 1943; originally with the medical corps, he later transferred to the Air Corps. He was trained at camps in Virginia, Florida, Nebraska, and New Mexico. He left San Francisco on Christmas Day of 1944 for overseas service.

He had been awarded two Bronze Stars and the good conduct medal; his unit had received a Presidential Unit Citation. (*Forest City Courier*, June 23, 1945)

Sergeant Gilbert was survived by his parents, Mr. and Mrs. J. T. Gilbert; a wife, Mrs. Ruth Gilbert; and two children. All are of Forest City.

Sergeant Gilbert was the last man of Rutherford County's missing service men to be reported on by the War Department. (*Forest City Courier*, June 6, 1946)

He is buried in the New Hope Methodist Cemetery, Polk County. (http://rfci.net/wdfloyd/)

Photo courtesy of <u>Daily Courier</u>, Forest City, North Carolina, and James R. Brown, Publisher

GILES, ROBERT E.
July 7, 1944

Robert E. Giles, Aviation Cadet of the U.S. Army Air Forces, expects to get his wings soon and sport a Lieutenant's bars on his shoulders. He is the son of Mr. and Mrs. J. H. Giles of Spindale. (*Forest City Courier*, Big Issue, August 12, 1943)

Lieutenant Robert E. Giles, 20, was the son of Mr. and Mrs. J. H. Giles of Spindale. He was reported missing in action over Germany since July 7, 1944. Lieutenant Giles (1924-1944) was in the U.S. Air Corps and had been overseas since June 14, 1944. The day he was reported missing was exactly 25 months from the date he entered service. He graduated at Central High School in the Class of 1941. Before going into service, Lieutenant Robert E. Giles was employed by the Stonecutter Mills of Spindale. (*Rutherford County News*, July 27, 1944)

Photo courtesy of <u>Daily Courier</u>, Forest City, North Carolina, and James R. Brown, Publisher

GODFREY, HARVEY HERMAN
January 1945

Harvey Herman Godfrey, Machinists Mate Second Class, U.S. Navy, was declared dead by the Navy Department. H. H. Godfrey (1915-1945) was reported missing in action in January. He was a son of Mr. and Mrs. Charles W. Godfrey of Spindale. His parents, two brothers in service, and two sisters survived him. (*Forest City Courier*, April 12, 1945)

GORDON, RALEIGH R.
January 15, 1945

Private First Class Raleigh R. Gordon, aged 21, son of Mr. and Mrs. Edward D. Gordon of the Floyds Creek Community, Mooresboro, Route 1, was killed in action in Arlon, Belgium on January 15, 1945. Trained at Camp Rucker, Alabama, and Camp Butner, North Carolina, he had served the U.S. Army overseas since May of 1944.

Private First Class Gordon (May 15, 1923-January 15, 1945) was survived by his parents; four brothers: Private Thomas Gordon with the First Army in Germany; Clyde Gordon, Bostic, Route 1; Bob Gordon, Rutherfordton, Route 1; and T. C. Gordon, at home; and six sisters: Private Etheleen Gordon, Women's Army Corps, stationed at Dill Field, Florida; Private Edna Gee, Women's Army Corps, Greenville Army Air Base, South Carolina; Mrs. W. B. Pearson; Mrs. T. C. Holland, Jr., Mooresboro, Route 1; Mrs. Dexter Pace, Saluda; and Mrs. Ada Gordon, at home. (*Forest City Courier*, February 8, 1945)

Photo courtesy of O'Lema Gordon Holland

GRANT, WOODROW WILSON
May 1, 1947 (1945)

Sergeant Woodrow Wilson Grant (September 15, 1912) is honored with a marker in the World War II Memorial Garden Section of the Cool Springs Cemetery. His dates are given as 1912-1945.

His remains are buried in the Avondale Cemetery with a marker reading September 15, 1912, and May 1, 1947. (http://rfci.net/wdfloyd/) He served his country and represented his county well during World War II.

GRAY, DANIEL EDWARDS
May 12, 1944

Private Daniel Edwards Gray, aged 20, of Rutherfordton, was killed in action in Italy on May 12, according to a message from the War Department to his mother, Mrs. Alice McBrayer Gray of Rutherfordton.

Private Gray's death brought Rutherford County's casualty list of World War II to 32 killed and four missing.

Private Gray entered the U.S. Army in February of 1943; he went overseas last January. A native of Chapel Hill, he was educated at Tar Heel High School, Bladen County, and Campbell College.

His mother received a letter from him dated May 9, 1944, saying not to expect many letters from him as he was "going into active duty."

Private Daniel Gray (August 30, 1923-May 12, 1944) was survived by his mother; a brother, Private Robert Gray, serving with the U.S. Army in Italy; a sister, Miss Jamie Gray of Rutherfordton; and his paternal grandparents Mr. and Mrs. W. W. Gray of this section. (*Forest City Courier*, June 15, 1944) He is buried in the Rutherfordton City Cemetery, Section #5. (http://rfci.net/wdfloyd/)

GREEN, DAVID L.
July 13, 1944

Staff Sergeant David L. Green*, son of Mr. and Mrs. Ralph V. Green of Forest City, Route 2, was killed in action in France on July 13, 1944, according to a message received Saturday. Staff Sergeant Green enlisted in the U.S. Army about two and one-half years before his death.

Staff Sergeant Green (October 2, 1922-July 13, 1944) was survived by his parents, Mr. and Mrs. Ralph Green; two brothers: Seaman First Class Clarence E. Green, Naval Base, Norfolk, Virginia; and Seaman Second Class Zeb Green of Jacksonville, Florida. (*Forest City Courier*, August 10, 1944) He is buried in the Bethany Baptist Cemetery. (http://rfci.net/wdfloyd/)

*Some sources spell his name as "Greene."

Photo courtesy of <u>Daily Courier</u>, Forest City, North Carolina, and James R. Brown, Publisher

GREENE, ELLIS P., JR.
October 30, 1944

Private Ellis P. Greene, Jr., son of the Reverend and Mrs. E. P. Greene of Harris, was killed in action in France on October 30, 1944, according to a message from the War Department.

Private Greene's death brought Rutherford County's total World War II toll to 70 dead, 11 missing, and 22 prisoners of war.

Private Greene (1924-1944) had been in the U.S. Army for 16 months. He landed in North Africa in November of 1943; spent eight months on the Anzio beachhead; and was moved to France in July of 1944.

His parents survived him. His father was pastor of the Broad River Methodist Circuit. He had three sisters: Mrs. Kenneth Clay, Lincolnton; Mrs. John H. Jenkins, Harris; and Mrs. Ralph E. Hudson of Lincoln County.

Three brothers-in-law were overseas; they were Private George Kenneth Clay, Corporal John H. Jenkins, and Seaman Second Class Ralph E. Hudson. (*Forest City Courier*, November 23, 1944)

GREENE, JAMES T.
July 9, 1944

Staff Sergeant James T. Greene, 26, son of G. W. Greene, Ellenboro, Route 2, was wounded in action in France, July 4, 1944. He went overseas last March and entered the U.S. Army in March, 1941. (*Rutherford County News*, August 10, 1944)

Staff Sergeant James Greene, aged 26, son of Mr. and Mrs. George Greene of the Oak Grove Community, Ellenboro, Route 2, died of wounds in a hospital July 9, according to a message received by his parents. Staff Sergeant Greene, U.S. Army, was seriously wounded July 4 in action in France and died five days later in a hospital. He would have been 26 years of age had he lived until August 17. His parents and several brothers and sisters survived him. (*Forest City Courier*, August 17, 1944)

A special memorial service was held Sunday morning at 11 o'clock for Staff Sergeant Greene (August 17, 1918-July 9, 1944) at Oak Grove Methodist Church, of which he was a member. The Reverend Van Harrison, the pastor, conducted the service, and Mr. C. A. Kennedy had charge of the music.

He was survived by his parents, Mr. and Mrs. G. W. Greene; six brothers: Walter of Avondale; Austin of Greer, South Carolina; Lewis of Welch Cove, North Carolina; Earl of Cliffside; Boyce and Morris Greene at home; and four sisters: Mrs. Ray Wilson, Mrs. Raymond Lindsay and Mrs. Reid Hamrick of Caroleen; and Miss Ila Greene at home. (*Forest City Courier*, August 17, 1944) He is buried in the Oak Grove Methodist Cemetery. (http://rfci.net/wdfloyd/)

On April 5, 1946, Mr. and Mrs. George Greene of Ellenboro accepted a posthumous Bronze Star Medal awarded to their son Staff Sergeant James T. Green by Major Fred Brillinger from Moore General Hospital.

Staff Sergeant Greene entered military service from Ellenboro on March 13, 1941. Besides his parents, two brothers (Maurice and Boyce) and a sister (Ila) survive the hero.

The citation reads:

Staff Sergeant James T. Greene 34031210, 120th Infantry Regiment, United States Army, is awarded the Bronze Star Medal for exceptionally meritorious conduct against the enemy on July 3 and 4, 1944, in France. Sergeant Greene was a member of a patrol whose mission was to enter enemy lines to capture or inflict casualties on the enemy. By his alertness and devotion to duty, Sergeant Greene contributed much to the success of the patrol. Though wounded by enemy fire, he displayed unusual ability and calmness, and the patrol was able to successfully perform its mission, killing four of the enemy and silencing an enemy machine gun. The actions of Sergeant Greene on this occasion reflect high credit on himself and the armed forces. Staff Sergeant Greene entered military service from North Carolina. (*Forest City Courier*, April 18. 1946)

Photo courtesy of Daily Courier, Forest City, North Carolina, and James R. Brown, Publisher

GRISWOLD, JOHN D.
August 1, 1943

World War II comes ever closer home. Monday the Adjutant General's office in Washington notified. . .W. M. Griswold and family of their son. . .

The wire to Mrs. Helen Griswold said:

> I regret to inform you that the Commanding General North Africa Area reports your son Private First Class John D. Griswold, missing in action since August 1. If further details or other information of his status are received, you will be promptly notified.

The Griswold family heard from John D., U.S. Army, in July. He had a brother, Corporal J. B. Griswold at Chanute Field, Ill. (*Rutherford County News*, September 9, 1943)

Mr. and Mrs. W. M. Griswold of Rutherfordton received a wire from the Commanding General on Tuesday. The message stated that their son Private First Class John D. Griswold (1920-1943) was killed in action on August 1 in North Africa. On September 6 the parents had had a wire from the War Department stating he was missing in action. (*Rutherford County News*, October 7, 1943)

GUFFEY, JOHN WILLIAM
March 22, 1945

Private First Class John William Guffey, 25, of the Oakland Community, Forest City, Route 1, was killed in action in Germany on March 22. A resident of the Oakland Community, near Spindale, Private First Class Guffey entered the U.S. Army in June of 1944; he received part of his training in Florida. He went overseas upon completion of his Florida training. He had been in Germany only a short time.

Private First Class Guffey (1920-1945) attended the schools at Oakland and Central High; after leaving high school, he was employed in one of the Spindale mills. He had been married four years and was survived by his wife Florence Guffey; one child, Madge; and his parents: Mr. and Mrs. John Guffey, who reside in the Oakland Community. (*Forest City Courier*, April 12, 1945)

Memorial services were held for Private First Class John William Guffey at Adaville Baptist Church Sunday, June 17, at 2 o'clock. He was killed in action on March 22, 1945.

Private First Class Guffey was born August 8, 1920, and graduated from Central High School in 1939. Surviving him were his parents; his wife; daughter, Madge, 2; four sisters: Mrs. Mary Sue Carver, Mrs. Cleo Greene, Mrs. Ola Hudson, and Mrs. Elsie Moore.

He was inducted into service July 12, 1944, trained at Camp Blanding, Florida, and went overseas in December of 1944. A member of an Infantry Regiment, he was killed in line of duty on German soil, March 22, eight months and ten days after he entered service.

Company 36, North Carolina State Guard, under command of Captain J. J. Tarlton, had charge of the service. The afternoon's program included "Faith of Our Fathers," sung by Adaville choir; scripture by the Reverend R. L. Crawford; prayer by the Reverend Charloe Walker; male quartet, by Dr. W. L. Stallings, W. C. Grayson, W. H. Fagan, Frank Smith;

memorial address, the Reverend Olen Kendrick; solo "Sunrise Tomorrow"; the Reverend Miller Freeman; benediction; Taps, D. C. Cole. (*Forest City Courier*, June 7, 1945) He is buried in the Adaville Baptist Church Cemetery. (http://rfci.net/wdfloyd/)

Photo courtesy of <u>Daily Courier</u>, Forest City, North Carolina, and James R. Brown, Publisher

GUNTER, L. WILBURN
October 9, 1944

Private L. Wilburn Gunter, aged 27, of Bostic, was killed in action in France October 9, according to a message received Tuesday by his wife, Mrs. Lenora Goforth Gunter of Bostic.

Private L. Wilburn Gunter was survived by his widow; three children: Tony, Barbara, and Judy; his parents, Mr. and Mrs. J. D. Gunter, all of Bostic; one brother, Staff Sergeant Max Gunter, U.S. Army, stationed at Moses Lake, Washington; and one sister, Mary Cathryn Gunter, Bostic.

A member of an U.S. Army Infantry Unit, he entered service on January 17, 1944, and went overseas in July of 1944. (*Forest City Courier*, November 2, 1944)

Photos courtesy of Judy Gunter Bridges

HALL, DANIEL KERP
January 25, 1945

Private Daniel Kerp Hall, 20, was reported missing in action in Luxembourg since January 25th. His parents, Mr. and Mrs. Gilkey A. Hall, Sr., of Union Mills, received the message. Of the U.S. Army, Private Hall was a brother of Private First Class Gilkey A. Hall, Jr., who was killed in action last June in Normandy. (*Forest City Courier*, February 22, 1945)

Private First Class Daniel K. Hall, Union Mills, Route 1, reported last week as being missing in action, was killed in action in Luxembourg on January 25. His parents, Mr. and Mrs. Gilkey A. Hall, Sr., of Union Mills, received the message.

Private First Class Hall was inducted into the U.S. Army on June 21, 1944, at Fort Bragg and completed his training at Camp Blanding, Florida. He was sent overseas from Fort Meade, Maryland. He served in France, Belgium, Germany, and Luxembourg. His remains have been permanently interred at Henri-Chappelle, U.S. Cemetery, Belgium. Private First Class Daniel K. Hall, Plot H, Row 14, Grave 37. Headstone: Cross. (*Courtesy of Ruth Rhodes*)

Private Hall (June 25, 1924-January 25, 1945) was a brother of Private First Class Gilkey A. Hall, Jr., who was killed in France on June 7, 1944. This was the third set of brothers from Rutherford County to be killed in action. The other brothers were Private First Class Broadus H. McKinney and Private Earl McKinncy, of Rutherford, Star Route, and Private Lynn Ruppe and Private First Class Toy Ruppe, of Cliffside.

His parents; three sisters: Ruth, Marie, and Carolyn Hall; and a brother, Virgil Hall, survived Private First Class Hall. (March 1, 1945) A memorial is set up at the Round Hill Baptist Cemetery, Section #2. (http://rfci.net/wdfloyd/)

HALL, GILKEY ADDIE, JR.
June 7, 1944

Private Gilkey Addie Hall, Jr., son of Gilkey Addie Hall, Sr., of near Union Mills, was reported missing in action in France, June 7, 1944. The message to his parents came last week. He entered the U.S. Army in September of 1942 and went overseas February of 1943. He was in the invasion of Sicily, North Africa, and France. The last letter his family had from him came early in June. He wrote the letter on May 27. (*Rutherford County News*, July 13, 1944)

A message Tuesday from the War Department stated that Gilkey Addie Hall, Jr. (1918-1944) was killed in action. (*Rutherford County News*, July 27, 1944)

Private Hall was known to his family and friends as "G.A." He was inducted into the Army on September 16, 1942, at Fort Bragg; he went from there to Camp Walters, Texas. He completed his training at Fort Meade, Maryland, and was sent overseas. He fought in North Africa, Tunisia, Sicily, Scotland, England, and France. His remains have been permanently interred at Henri-Chapelle, U.S. Military Cemetery, Belgium. Private First Class Gilkey Addie Hall, Jr., Plot H. Row 14, Grave 28. Headstone: Cross.

(Courtesy of Ruth Rhodes)

HANCOCK, WALTER S.
July 13, 1944

Sunday, Private Walter S. Hancock of Gilkey was reported killed in action in Italy, July 13, 1944. He went overseas in March and had been in the U.S. Army for fifteen months. Private Hancock (1921-1944) was born and reared in Spindale; he was a son of the late Mr. William Hancock. His wife, the former Miss Marie Fincannon, resided with her parents, Mr. and Mrs. C. D. Fincannon of Gilkey. They have an eight-month-old son that Private Hancock (1921-1944) never saw. His widow and son; four brothers; and two sisters survived him. (*Forest City Courier*, August 10, 1944)

Photo courtesy of Daily Courier, Forest City, North Carolina, and James R. Brown, Publisher

HARDIN, EDWARD J., SR.
April 9, 1945

Edward J. Hardin, Sr., Construction Mechanic Third Class, U.S. Navy Seabees, died of bronchial pneumonia Monday afternoon at 2:30 o'clock in a naval hospital in San Francisco. A son of Mrs. Will Hardin and the late Sheriff Hardin, Construction Mechanic, Third Class Hardin (September 3, 1912-April 9, 1945) had been in the Seabees since 1942. He was 32 years of age.

The body was shipped from San Francisco to Rutherfordton where funeral services were held upon its arrival. Hardin spent several years in the United States Army prior to entering the U.S. Navy. He had recently spent 23 months overseas and had lately arrived in the United States. He was scheduled for a leave of absence to visit home when he died.

He was survived by his wife, the former Margaret Walker, of Rutherfordton; two small sons, William and Edward; his mother, Mrs. W. C. Hardin, of Rutherfordton; four sisters: Mrs. J. H. Williams, Rutherfordton, Star Route; Mrs. W. J. McEntire, Spindale; Mrs. Hope Harrill, Forest City; and Mrs. Alton Dotson, of Radford, VA; and two brothers: Curtis Hardin and Calvin Hardin, the latter in the U.S. Army and serving in Europe at the time of Edward Hardin's death. (*Forest City Courier*, April 12, 1945) He is buried in the Rutherfordton Cemetery, Section #5. (http://rfci.net/wdfloyd/)

HARMON, OTHA L.
June 16, 1944

Private First Class Otha L. Harmon, son of Mr. and Mrs. G. T. Harmon of Gaffney, Route 3, near Cliffside, died June 16, 1944, from wounds received June 9, 1944, on the North Burma front. (*Rutherford County News*, August 3, 1944)

His wife, Mrs. Mary Simmons Harmon, received the message from the War Department. Private Harmon (1921-1944) entered the U.S. Army on November 9, 1942, and went overseas in September of 1943. He was a member of Prospect Baptist Church. His parents, five sisters, and six brothers survived him. The brothers were Staff Sergeant Russell W. Harmon of Fort Lewis, Washington; Seaman First Class Ulysses E. Harmon of Charleston; Wayne, George, Wiseman, and Alfred Harmon. The sisters were Miss Marie Harmon, Mrs. Grady Hammett, Mrs. Charlie Godfrey, Mrs. Taft Cobb, and Mrs. C. B. Beason. *(Courtesy of Alfred Harmon)*

Photo courtesy of Alfred Harmon

HARRILL, JAMES WILBUR
December 25, 1945

Sergeant James Wilbur Harrill, aged 21, son of Mr. and Mrs. E. Yates Harrill of Avondale, was killed in an automobile wreck in England on December 25, according to a message received from the War Department by his parents.

Funeral services for young Harrill were held in England, according to the message.

Sergeant Harrill (October 9, 1923-December 25, 1945) was a graduate of Tri-High School and had been active in school circles. He had been in service about three years and had been overseas about two and one-half years. He was expected to arrive home soon. His parents survived him; he was the only child. (*Rutherford County News*, January 10, 1946)

He had entered service on December 3, 1942, and had been overseas 25 months at the time of his death. His commanding officer gave the following details in a letter to the parents:

> Sergeant Harrill was assigned to this Station Motor Pool at 8th Fighter Command as a mechanic, but had also been driving for the station at various times. On Christmas night he left this station driving a command car for an officer enroute to a town near London. The weather was unsettled and the highway was wet and slippery as a consequence. From the story of the officer whom Sergeant Harrill was driving, it appears that the vehicle skidded when it struck a pool of water on the highway; when Sergeant Harrill swung the steering wheel to offset the skid, the vehicle turned over after striking the curbing at the edge of the road. Sergeant Harrill was instantly killed, and the officer accompanying him seriously injured. The body was brought to this station and prepared for burial, and this afternoon (December 28) a military funeral was held at Brookside American Military Cemetery, near Cambridge, and about 30

miles from this station. Lieutenant Carl Adams of this squadron and a large group of Sergeant Harrill's friends attended the funeral, which was conducted by Chaplain Warner of the 8th Fighter Command with full military honors, including a color guard, guard of honor, and a firing squad. (*Forest City Courier*, January 31, 1946)

Funeral services for Sergeant James W. Harrill, 22, were held at the Avondale Methodist Church. Interment was in the Oak Grove Methodist Church Cemetery.

Sergeant Harrill took his basic training at Jefferson Barracks, Missouri, Ordnance School, and at an Ordnance School in Atlanta, Georgia, and Venice, Florida. He was sent overseas on November 4, 1943, and was attached to the ordnance Division of the Eighth Air Force.

Information and photographs courtesy of Jerrell Bedford

HARRILL, OMAR RAY
August 18, 1943

Omar Ray Harrill, Cliffside, of the U.S. Navy, was reported missing in action. His parents, Mr. and Mrs. A. M. Harrill of near Cliffside, were notified by the Navy Department of this fact last week. Omar entered the U.S. Navy in March of 1943. His parents received no details of the action. (*Forest City Courier*, September 23, 1943)

Omar Ray Harrill (October 10, 1923-August 18, 1943) was reported dead after being classified as missing for a period of one year. He was reported missing in August of 1943 when his ship sank. (*Forest City Courier*, September 14, 1944) His memorial is in the Bethel Baptist Church Cemetery, Ellenboro. (http://rfci.net/wdfloyd/)

Photos courtesy of <u>Daily Courier</u>, Forest City, North Carolina, and James R. Brown, Publisher

HARRIS, DUREN C.
January 19, 1945

Technical Sergeant Five Duren C. Harris (August 31, 1920-January 19, 1945), son of Mr. and Mrs. J. S. Harris, of the Broad River Church Community, Rutherfordton, Route 1, was killed on January 19 in action on Luzon in the South Pacific, according to a message received by the parents. He had been in the U.S. Army about a year.

He took his training at Camp Grant, Illinois; Camp Rice, California; and San Francisco, California. He served in Australia, New Guinea, and Luzon. His parents and several brothers and sisters survived him. (*Forest City Courier*, March 22, 1945/Jeanette Dills and Virgie Harris)

Technical Sergeant Five Duren C. Harris entered the U.S. Army on August 26, 1942. He had spent 18 months overseas. (*Jeanette Dills and Virgie Harris*)

The oldest of 10 children, Technical Sergeant Five Duren C. Harris came home in the autumn of 1947. His final place of interment was Greenriver Baptist Church, 2880 Ken Miller Road, Rutherfordton, North Carolina 28139. (*Jeanette Dills and Virgie W. Harris*)

Photo courtesy of <u>Daily Courier</u>, Forest City, North Carolina, James R. Brown, Publisher, Virgie Harris and Jeanette Dills.

HARRIS, HULAND T.
November 14, 1944

Staff Sergeant Huland T. Harris, of the Montford Cove Community, Union Mills, Route 2, was officially declared dead since November 14, 1944, when he and his crew failed to return to their base at Dover, Delaware, following a training flight.

A son of Mr. and Mrs. L. V. Harris of Montford Cove, Sergeant Harris (1921-1944), U.S. Army Air Forces, was survived by two sisters, Mrs. Horace Norton and Miss Jean Harris, of Marion; three brothers: Ward Harris, Wilmington; First Sergeant Dodd Harris of Camp Polk, Louisiana; and Staff Sergeant Hoyt Harris, who was in New Guinea.

Details of Sergeant Harris's death are given in a letter to the parents from the commandant of the Dover Army Air Base, Colonel Edwin Dixon.

Dear Mr. Harris:

As Commanding Officer of this station of which your son, Staff Sergeant Huland T. Harris, was a member, it becomes my sorrowful duty to extend the heartfelt condolences of each officer and man of my command to you, his father, at this time of your great bereavement.

Your son was very popular with the officers and men of this station. His efficiency as a soldier marked him as a true gentleman in every sense of the word, and his death was a tremendous shock to each of us.

On the 14th of November, 1944 your son departed from this station in an army airplane on an administrative flight and training flight for Olmstead Field, Pennsylvania. On the same day this airplane departed from Olmstead Field and failed to return to this station. Immediately after this airplane was presumed missing, airplanes from bases on the East Coast were in the air searching for any trace of the missing plane. In addition to this, the United States Coast Guard was informed to be on the lookout for the signs of an aircraft that may have been forced down while over the sea, and a general warning was issued to all State Police of nearby states. I can assure you, Mr. Harris, that everything humanly possible was done to locate this missing plane.

This search was continued until the 25th day of November, 1944. As nothing was reported of the missing plane, it was decided to abandon the search and carry your son on the rolls of the United States Army as missing.

On the 12th day of January this year, I received a written report from the Commanding General, First Air Force, concerning a subsequent search and discovery of evidence of this missing plane at Port Norris, New Jersey. Oyster fishermen off shore in Delaware Bay discovered metal parts of an army airplane. An army crash boat was immediately dispatched to the scene of this discovery. Grappling operations revealed no further evidence of bodies of the missing crew.

The metal parts found were thoroughly examined by army authorities, and were adequately identified as being pieces of the missing plane. In view of this conclusive evidence that was discovered, your son was dropped from the rolls of the army as being carried in a missing status and was pronounced officially dead as of 14 November 1944. (*Forest City Courier*, February 15, 1945)

HARRIS, WALLACE LONZO
June 20, 1945

Private Wallace Lonzo Harris, aged 23, a member of the United States Marine Corps, was killed in action on Okinawa on June 20, 1945, according to a report received from the War Department by his wife, Mrs. Harris, in Rutherfordton.

Private Harris's death brought Rutherford County's total World War II casualties to 117 dead, 16 missing, and four prisoners of war.

Private Harris (1922-1945) entered service June 8, 1944, and was overseas two months at the time of his death. His wife and a daughter, Elizabeth Ann, survived him. (*Rutherford County News*, July 12, 1945)

HARSTIN, HUGH G.
February 10, 1944

Private Hugh Harstin, 22, was a former employee of the Cleghorn Mills, spinning department. He had been overseas nearly two years before being killed in action in the Fiji Islands. It was thought he was in action against the Japanese. He enlisted in the U.S. Army on February 19, 1941. (*Rutherford County News*, February 24, 1944)

Private Hugh G. Harstin (1920-1944) was the son of Mr. and Mrs. G. W. Harstin of Rutherfordton and Gastonia. The first report was that he was killed in action February 10 in the Fiji Islands. Later it was reported he was injured riding a motorcycle and died soon afterwards in a hospital. Full details were not given. He was 22 years old and had been overseas nearly two years. (*Rutherford County News*, March 16, 1944)

Photo courtesy of <u>Daily Courier</u>, Forest City, North Carolina, and James R. Brown, Publisher

HARVEY, ARTHUR J.
May 26, 1944

Private First Class Arthur J. Harvey died of wounds received May 26 in Italy, according to a wire from Washington, D.C., last week to his mother, Mrs. Lillie Harvey at the Cleghorn Mills here. Private First Class Harvey (1922-1944) had been overseas 16 months. He entered the service November of 1942. He was wounded last February. He was a native of the Cedar Creek section and was the son of the late William Harvey. His widow and a child, born after he entered the U.S. Army, survived him. His wife Maxine Harvey resided in Glenwood with her parents, Mr. and Mrs. Anderson Romine. Harvey worked at the Cleghorn Mills before entering the service. He was also survived by four sisters: Mrs. Ossie Dillingham, a twin of the deceased; Mrs. Edna Arrowood; Mrs. Ellen Arrowood, Rutherfordton; and Mrs. Maude Beachboard of Marion; and a brother, Edward Harvey, Gastonia. (*Rutherford County News*, January 29, 1944)

HAWKINS, HAROLD L.
December 1943

Mr. and Mrs. George T. Hawkins of Alexander Rural Station, Forest City, received from Marine Headquarters in Washington a telegram informing them of the death of their son. He was killed in action; the telegram requested that his station and date of death not be divulged.

Harold L. Hawkins (1924-1943) volunteered for service in the U.S. Marine Corps on September 19, 1942. He was trained at New River Marine Base and at Parris Island, South Carolina. From there he went to Camp Elliott, California, but he was soon transferred to Camp Pendleton, California. He embarked from California for overseas service. He had been overseas since March.

His parents; one sister, Mrs. Marie Bailey of Charlotte; and four brothers—Private Lawrence Hawkins, Camp Adair, Oregon; Sergeant Geo. T. Hawkins, Camp Carson, Colorado; and Earl and Roy Hawkins, at home—survived him. (*Forest City Courier*, January 13, 1944)

HAWKINS, WILLIAM GRADY, SR.
July 11, 1944

Mrs. William Grady Hawkins of Rutherfordton received a wire Saturday from Washington stating that her husband, Staff Sergeant Williams Grady Hawkins, Sr., 34, was killed in action in France on July 11. Staff Sergeant Hawkins went overseas last April after being trained for the U.S. Army at Camp Atterbury, Indiana, and Camp Breckenridge, Kentucky. He served in England and was in the invasion of France.

Staff Sergeant Hawkins (1920-1944) was survived by his widow; a son, W. G. Hawkins, Jr., age 4; parents, Mr. and Mrs. W. D. Hawkins, all of Rutherfordton; and the following brothers and sisters: Mrs. Harland Bailey; Sergeant Grover F. Hawkins, Camp Campbell, Kentucky; Misses Grace, Janet and Dorcus Hawkins; Mrs. Horace Atchely; Sidney Claude Hawkins, Seaman Second Class, then in Italy; and W. D. Hawkins, Jr. (*Rutherford County News*, August 10, 1944)

HINES, CLYDE, JR.
1944

Private First Class Clyde Hines, Jr., U.S. Army, died in 1944. Private First Class Hines (1907-1944) was from Rutherfordton and served Rutherford County well.

HODGE, CHARLES W., JR.
October 6, 1944

Private Charles V. Hodge, Jr., son of Mr. and Mrs. C. W. Hodge of near Rutherfordton, was killed in action in France on October 6, 1944, according to a message received from the War Department.

A member of an Infantry Regiment of the U.S. Army, Private Hodge (1917-1944) had been overseas only two months when killed.

His widow, the former Miss Gertie McGuinn of Rutherfordton; their five-year-old daughter; his parents, Mr. and Mrs. Charles W. Hodge of near Rutherfordton; three brothers; and five sisters survived him. (*Forest City Courier*, November 2, 1944)

HODGE, FRANK L.
August 11, 1943

Private Frank L. Hodge, the youngest son of Mr. and Mrs. Spain Hodge of near Rutherfordton, was killed in action, North African area, August 11, according to a message from the War Dept. last week. Private Hodge was 22 years old. He entered the U.S. Army on November 17, 1942, and went overseas about March 1943. His last letter to his family was dated August 2 from Sicily. He wrote he liked Sicily better than Africa and found lemons, tomatoes, and melons in Sicily. (*Rutherford County News*, September 16, 1943)

World War II comes ever closer home. Monday the Adjutant General's Office in Washington notified Spain Hodge and family of their son.

The message to Mr. and Mrs. Hodge read:

The Secretary of War desires that I tender his deep sympathy to you in the loss of your son Private Frank L. Hodge. Reports received state that he was killed in action on August 11, in North African Area. Letter follows. (*Rutherford County News*, September 13, 1944)

Private Hodge (May 4, 1921-August 11, 1943) was survived by his parents; three brothers, J. Thomas Hodge, Alexandria, Virginia; Curtis Hodge, Mt. Vernon section; and Claude Hodge, at the home place. He had four surviving sisters: Mildred Rippy, at the home place; Mrs. Maude Vickers, this section; Velcie Mae Flynn, Uree section; and Betty Jean Hodge at home.

The family desires that his body be brought home after the war ends. (*Rutherford County News*, September 16, 1943) He is buried in the Piedmont Baptist Cemetery. (http://rfci.net/wdfloyd/)

Photo on previous page courtesy of <u>Daily Courier</u>, Forest City, North Carolina, and James R. Brown, Publisher

Information and photograph courtesy of Maude Hodge Vickers

HOLLIFIELD, JOSEPH DWIGHT
July 4, 1944

Private First Class Joseph Dwight Hollifield, 22, son of Thomas Hollifield, was killed July 4, 1944, in France. His father; brother Rex Hollifield, Augusta, Georgia; and two sisters: Mrs. Dorcas Melton, Ellenboro, Route 1; and Miss Madge Hollifield of Washington, D.C., survived him. Private First Class Hollifield (1922-1944) of the U.S. Army was originally from Bostic. (*Rutherford County News*, August 3, 1944)

HOUSER, VERNON T.
March 4, 1942

Messrs. Thurman F. and C. C. Houser were called to New Orleans, Louisiana, last Thursday on account of the serious illness of Vernon Houser, their brother, who had been in a Marine hospital for some time. As this was written, little had been heard from them. Outside communication was out of order and only mails via railroad were coming through. (*Rutherford County News*, March 5, 1942)

Mr. Vernon T. Houser, 37, native of Rutherfordton, died last Wednesday in a U.S. Marine Hospital in New Orleans, Louisiana, where he had been a patient for fourteen months.

His body arrived here Friday. Funeral services were held at the Keeter Mortuary Saturday morning with the Reverend C. N. Royal, Pastor of the First Baptist Church, in charge. Burial followed here in the city cemetery. His grave was covered with beautiful flowers.

Mr. Houser had been in the military service of his country for nearly 20 years. He was retired during his illness. Two of his brothers, C. C. and Thurman F. Houser, were with him when he died. They were called there several days ago, when he became critically ill.

Mr. Houser enjoyed a wide circle of friends. He made good in the service of his country. He was survived by his widow and a four and one-half year old daughter; his parents, Mr. and Mrs. R. L. Houser of Rutherfordton; three sisters: Mrs. Lloyd Hensley of near Rutherfordton; Mrs. N. E. Aydlet, Elizabeth City; Mrs. Frank Armfield of Decatur, Georgia; and three brothers: C. C. and Worth Houser of Rutherfordton; and Thurman F. Houser, Asheville. (*Rutherford County News*, March 12, 1942)

Vernon Houser (December 16, 1906-March 4, 1942) of Rutherfordton, aged 36, of the U.S. Marine Corps, died in New Orleans Marine Hospital March 4, 1942. His body was returned to Rutherfordton for interment. He was a son of Mr. and Mrs. R. L. Houser. He had spent about 20 years in the Marine Corps. (*Forest City Courier*, August 12, 1945) He is buried in the Rutherfordton City Cemetery, Section #1. (http://rfci.net/wdfloyd/)

HUFFSTICKLER, HORACE RAY
January 18, 1945

Five Brothers Served Their Country with Distinction.

Sergeant Curtis Huffstickler   *Corporal Albert Woodrow Huffstickler*   *Private Horace R. Huffstickler*

Sergeant Curtis Huffstickler was overseas and saw action in the invasion of Africa and Sicily. He was wounded in Sicily and spent some time in a hospital and had not gone back on active duty. He entered the U.S. Army in June of 1941 and received his basic training at Fort Knox, Kentucky. He was the son of E. E. Huffstickler of Rutherfordton. Before entering the U.S. Army, he was employed in the Stonecutter Mills at Spindale.

Corporal Albert Woodrow Huffstickler was on duty somewhere in Louisiana. He entered the armed forces August 11 at Fort Jackson, South Carolina, and took his basic training at Camp Wolters, Texas, before going to Louisiana. He was another son of E. E. Huffstickler. He was married August 14 of this year to Miss Beulah Godfrey of Spindale. Mrs. Huffstickler made her home with her parents, Mr. and Mrs. Charley Godfrey in Spindale.

Private Horace R. Huffstickler, son of Mr. E. E. Huffstickler, was in an embarkation camp in New York when family last heard from him. He entered the armed forces March 9, 1943, and received his training at Fort Jackson, South Carolina, and Fort Meade, Maryland. He graduated from the Rutherfordton-Spindale High School in the class of 1942; at the time he was drafted, the Doncaster Collar and Shirt Company in Rutherfordton employed him. (*Rutherford County News*, November 25, 1943)

Sergeant Ilus L. Huffstickler served with the State Guard Unit of Rutherford County. He did his part by helping keep the home front ready. He was married and had three children; his wife was the former Miss Francis Dalton. Stonecutter Mills at Spindale employed him.

Coleman E. Huffstickler served on the Richmond Police Force. He was married and had two children.

The Death of Private First Class Horace Ray Huffstickler

Sergeant Ilus L.   *Coleman E. Huffstickler*
Huffstickler

Private First Class Horace Ray Huffstickler, son of Mr. and Mrs. E. E. Huffstickler of Spindale, died on January 18 from wounds received in action in France on January 12, according to a message from the War Department to his family, which they received Tuesday. They were notified several days ago that he had been wounded.

Private First Class Huffstickler (August 12, 1923-January 18, 1945) entered the U.S. Army in 1943, trained at Ft. Jackson, and was sent overseas in February 1944. He was in the Infantry and took part in the invasion of Italy.

A graduate of Central High School, he was employed for some time by Doncaster Shirt Company and by Hill's Barbecue for a short time prior to his enlistment. His parents, eight half-brothers, and eight half-sisters survived him. He was 21 years old. (*Forest City Courier*, February 8, 1945) He is buried in the Rutherfordton City Cemetery, Section #4. (http://rfci.net/wdfloyd/)

Photos courtesy of <u>Daily Courier</u>, Forest City, North Carolina, and James R. Brown, Publisher

HUMPHRIES, SHUFORD NATHANIEL
June 11, 1944

Private First Class Shuford Nathaniel Humphries of Spindale was reported missing in action since June 11, 1944. He was a Paratrooper and received his basic training at Camp Wheeler, Georgia, and his Paratroop Training at Fort Benning, Georgia. He went overseas last December. His parents live in Florida, formerly in Spindale. Mrs. Humphries, the former Miss Mabel Wilson, lives with her stepmother, Mrs. J. N. Wilson in Spindale. He entered the service in May of 1942. (*Forest City Courier*, February 8, 1945)

Photo courtesy of <u>Daily Courier</u>, Forest City, North Carolina, and James R. Brown, Publisher

Mr. and Mrs. W. L. Humphries of Forest City, Route 2, received word that their son, Private First Class Shuford Humphries, aged 26, missing since June 11, 1944, was dead.

Private First Class Humphries (April 26, 1916-June 11, 1944) was a member of the Paratroopers who landed in France shortly after the invasion on June 6. He was reported missing in action on June 11. The War Department confirms his death as having occurred on that date. He entered the U.S. Army two years ago, shortly after graduating from Mt. Vernon High School, and went overseas in October of 1943.

He was survived by his wife, Mrs. Mabel Wilson Humphries, of Spartanburg; his parents, Mr. and Mrs. W. L. Humphries of Forest City, Route 2, and Deland, Florida; two sisters: Mrs. Louise Street of Alexander, Mrs. Paul Crowder, Forest City, Route 2; two brothers, Foye Humphries of Spindale and Wilmer Humphries of Deland, Florida. (*Forest City Courier*, December 14, 1945)

Private First Class Humphries died at Normandy Beach; his sister Cleo Humphries Grose was able to visit his grave. He remained a Private First Class by choice.

Photo and information courtesy of Mrs. Cleo H. Grose

HUNT, GEORGE A.
August 12, 1943

Word was received in the county that Staff Sergeant George A. Hunt, U.S. Army Air Corps, had been missing in action since August 12, when he flew over Germany. His wife, Mrs. Edith Hunt, received the message Friday. Staff Sergeant Hunt was a gunner on a Flying Fortress stationed in England. He entered service September 4, 1942, and had been overseas three months. They were married December 25, 1941. He was the son of Mr. and Mrs. A. H. Hunt, formerly of Forest City, located in Portsmouth, Virginia, where Mr. Hunt was in defense work. (*Rutherford County News*, August 26, 1943)

Rutherford County's seventeenth casualty of World War II was reported here Saturday when Mrs. Edith Hunt received word that her husband, Staff Sergeant George A. Hunt, had been missing in action since August 12 over Gelsenkirchen, Germany. He was a gunner on a Flying Fortress and stationed in England.

Staff Sergeant and Mrs. Hunt were married on Christmas Day, 1941, and they have one daughter, Sandra, 11 months old. He entered the service on September 4, 1942, and had been overseas about three months. He was the son of Mr. and Mrs. A. H. Hunt of Forest City, who were living in Portsmouth, Virginia; Mr. Hunt was employed in a war industry.

Staff Sergeant Hunt was Forest City's third casualty and the seventeenth from Rutherford County. (*Forest City Courier*, August 20, 1943)

A later article simply stated: Sergeant George Hunt, killed August 12, 1943, son of Mr. and Mrs. A. H. Hunt and husband of Mrs. Edith Hunt, Forest City. (*Forest City Courier*, December 16, 1943)

Photo courtesy of <u>Daily Courier</u>, Forest City, North Carolina, and James R. Brown, Publisher

INGLE, HOWARD M.
September 12, 1945

Last rites for Private Howard M. Ingle, 29, of Spindale, were held at Caroleen Baptist Church Friday afternoon at 4 o'clock. The Reverend R. M. Hagler, pastor of the church, officiated. The Reverend C. C. Matheny of Spindale and the Reverend Joe Parson of Shelby assisted him. Interment was in the Oak Grove Methodist Church Cemetery.

Private Ingle (1916-1945) died instantly when a train hit the car that he was driving at Nebo in McDowell County late Tuesday night, September 11, or early morning, September 12. In company with a young lady, Private Ingle drove the car onto a blind crossing at Nebo. The young lady was uninjured although Private Ingle was killed.

He had spent 23 months overseas in the U.S. Army, had returned to the United States just a short time before, and had spent about half of his 30-days' leave at home, before reporting to a relocation center.

His mother, Mrs. Ike Ingle, of Spindale; three brothers: Miland and Will Ingle of Spindale, and J. T. Ingle of the U.S. Army; and two sisters survived him. (*Forest City Courier*, September 20, 1945)

JACKSON, ERNEST
1944

Ernest Jackson of the U.S. Army gave his life in 1944 in service of his country. He was formerly a resident of Union Mills.

(Courtesy of Nancy Stallcup's Memorial Gardens Honor Roll)

JACKSON, GUS J.
1943

Gus J. Jackson of the U.S. Army gave his life during World War II. Jackson (1920-1943) was from Forest City, North Carolina. *(Nancy Stallcup's Memorial Honor Roll)*

JACKSON, JAMES WILLIAM
June 13, 1944

James William Jackson, 22, son of Dewey Jackson of the Mill Spring section, was reported killed in action, June 13, 1944, in France. According to the message from the Secretary of War, Private First Class Jackson had been in the U.S. Army for about two years and had been overseas for three months. (*Rutherford County News*, July 13, 1944)

JEFFRIES, MONTRO
July 15, 1944

The soldier Montro Jeffries of Spindale, son of Verlon and Ossie Jeffries, died July 15, 1944, in Bristol, England. Verlon Jeffries worked for the town of Spindale; his son Montro Jeffries (January 20, 1918-July 15, 1944) was in the U.S. Army. The message came Monday to Ossie Jeffries. (*Rutherford County News*, July 27, 1944) His marker is in the Cool Springs Cemetery, Section #2. (http://rfci.net/wdfloyd/)

JENKINS, JOHN T.
December 24, 1944

Private First Class John T. Jenkins, 19, was killed in action in Belgium on December 24, 1944, according to a message received by his wife, Mrs. Maggie Quentin Jenkins, also of Forest City.

Private First Class Jenkins (1925-1944) entered the U.S. Army on May 13, 1944, and went overseas in October of 1944, as a member of a U.S. Army Infantry Regiment.

He was survived by his parents, Mr. and Mrs. E. D. Jenkins of Forest City; his wife; five brothers: Private Charles H. Jenkins, in Italy; Private First Class Orras Jenkins, with the U.S. Army in Germany; James Robert Jenkins, Roy Jenkins, and Stoney Jenkins, all of Forest City; and two sisters: Beth Ann and Edith Jenkins, at home. (*Forest City Courier*, January 18, 1945)

JOHNSON, DAVID COY
March 15, 1945

Staff Sergeant David Coy Johnson, aged 24, was killed in action March 15, 1945, somewhere in Germany. He was a son of John Johnson and the late Mrs. Johnson of Union Mills, Route 2. He entered service in 1942; took his training at Camp Van Dorn, Mississippi, and Camp Maxey, Texas, and went overseas last October as a member of the 99th Infantry Division of the First Army.

Staff Sergeant Johnson (April 13, 1920-March 15, 1945) was survived by his wife, the former Miss Callie Gladden of Charlotte, and of Route 1; his father, J. H. Johnson of Route 2; four sisters: Mrs. Earl (Roxie) Hutchins of Bostic, Route 1; Mrs. Broadus (Mittie) Hutchins, Rutherfordton, Route 2; Mrs. Rex (Lucy) Walters, Rutherfordton, and Miss Pauline Johnson at home; and four brothers: Corporal Henry B. Johnson, somewhere in Germany; Sergeant James R. Johnson, wounded twice and recuperating somewhere in France in a hospital; Corporal Junior

Johnson, somewhere in the South Pacific; and Jessie L. Johnson of Charlotte, who served two years and 4 months in the Army Air Corps, prior to his medical discharge. (*Forest City Courier*, April 12, 1945) Prior to his induction, Staff Sergeant Johnson was employed by the Hudson Hosiery Mills. He was 24 years old and was born in Rutherford County. Until his marriage to the former Miss Collie Gladden of Wilson Grove Section, he lived with his brother Jesse Johnson of 1116 Parkwood Avenue.

Photograph courtesy of Ethel Johnson and Helen Prince

Daily Courier, Forest City, North Carolina, and James R. Brown, Publisher

Courtesy of Helen Prince

IN GRATEFUL MEMORY OF

David C. Johnson

WHO DIED IN THE SERVICE OF HIS COUNTRY AT

in the European Area, March 15, 1945.

HE STANDS IN THE UNBROKEN LINE OF PATRIOTS WHO HAVE DARED TO DIE

THAT FREEDOM MIGHT LIVE, AND GROW, AND INCREASE ITS BLESSINGS.

FREEDOM LIVES, AND THROUGH IT, HE LIVES—

IN A WAY THAT HUMBLES THE UNDERTAKINGS OF MOST MEN

Franklin D. Roosevelt

PRESIDENT OF THE UNITED STATES OF AMERICA

Courtesy of Helen Prince

Photo of Grave in Belgium
Information courtesy of Helen Prince

Letter from Family in Belgium
Courtesy of Helen Prince

Froidthier July 28th

Dear Friend,

To-day it is sunday and I have little time to write to you. We've still have a load of troubles with my father but now he feels a little better. I hope that your mother is all right now and that you're working again.

Dear friend I went to the cemetery and I've put some flowers on David's grave. I've took some pictures too.

Now I've to tell you something they will transfer all the soldiers to America. They started yesterday next week the cemetery is closed for all the civilians because they have to transfer all the bodies. In the newspaper they says that you will have your husband for October.

In few more months you will pray on David's grave and O! hope that you will be very courageous.

Now I close and hope to get news from you very soon and your friends from Belgium send you a big hello.

Jacques Elise.

JONES, HOWARD L.
November 1, 1943

Private Howard L. Jones, son of Mr. and Mrs. C. M. "Bud" Jones of Forest City was killed in action in Italy on November 1, 1943. News of his death reached here last week. He was a member of an Infantry Regiment attached to the U.S. Fifth Army. (*Forest City Courier*, December 2, 1943)

The death of Private Howard L. Jones (1922-1943) brought Rutherford County's casualty list of World War II to 25 dead and four missing.

Private Jones enlisted in the U.S. Army on December 27, 1942. He had been overseas about three months, having landed in North Africa the latter part of July.

The telegram from the War Department, received here Tuesday morning, stated that he was killed in action in Italy on November 1.

His parents, one sister and five brothers, three of whom were in the U.S. Army, survived him. They were Private Carl Jones, Fort Jackson, South Carolina; Tim Jones and Joe Jones, Forest City; Private D. Bunyan Jones, Fort McClellan, Alabama; Private Odus Jones, Tuscaloosa, Alabama; and Mrs. Ruth White, Forest City.

Howard was a member of the infantry and was attached to the U.S. Fifth Army. (*Forest City Courier*, November 25, 1943)

Mr. and Mrs. C. M. Jones have been advised by the War Department that the Silver Star will be presented posthumously to their son Private Howard L. Jones who was killed in action last October in Italy.

The last message to Mr. and Mrs. Jones follows:

> I have the honor to inform you that, by direction of the President, the Silver Star decoration has been awarded posthumously to your son, Private Howard L. Jones, Infantry. The citation relating to this award was as follows:
>
> For gallantry in action on . . . October, 1943, in the vicinity of Italy. While on reconnaissance patrol with another soldier, Private Jones discovered a group of approximately six enemy

soldiers guarding a bridge in enemy-held territory. With utter disregard for his own personal safety, Private Jones and his fellow comrade advanced while under enemy fire and drove the enemy from the bridge before they could destroy it. . . . The courage and devotion to duty of Private Jones in the face of grave danger was exemplary and a credit to the armed forces of the United States.

The ceremony Sunday afternoon will be open to the public. The Purple Heart had been awarded the family on behalf of Private Jones some months ago. (*Forest City Courier*, May 11, 1944)

The Silver Star, high military decoration, was posthumously awarded to Private Howard L. Jones of Forest City. It was formally presented to his father, Columbus M. (Bud) Jones, and to Mrs. Jones by Colonel Frank W. Wilson, commanding officer of the Moore General Hospital, Sunday afternoon at 2 o'clock.

The presentation ceremony occurred at the home of the youth's parents in Forest City; a large number of friends and neighbors were present to witness the ceremony.

Private Jones, who was 20 years old, was killed in action in Italy in October of 1943, and the award was "For gallantry in action," in which he lost his life.

Captain Fred Killman, of the Moore General Hospital, read the citation, while the color guard advanced and remained at attention while the citation ceremony was observed.

Major G. F. Steele, also of Moore General Hospital, participated in the ceremony. Following the reading of the citation, Colonel Wilson advanced, pinned the medal on Mr. Jones, and made a short presentation speech.

The color guard was composed of Technical Sergeant Four John S. Devick, Corporal Maurice J. Lambert, and Private First Class Maurice J. Morrissette. Also accompanying the guard of honor was Sergeant Ernest Coffey, whose home was in Forest City.

The Silver Star was awarded posthumously to Private Jones by the citation, which reads in part:

> While on reconnaissance patrol with another soldier, Private Jones discovered a group of approximately six enemy soldiers guarding a bridge in enemy-held territory. With utter disregard for his own personal safety, Private Jones and his fellow comrade advanced while under enemy fire and drove the enemy from the bridge before they could destroy it . . . The courage and devotion

to duty of Private Jones in the face of grave danger was exemplary and a credit to the armed forces of the United States.

Mr. and Mrs. Jones were notified by the War Department last month that the posthumous award would be made.

Private Jones, who enlisted in the infantry December 27, 1942, had been overseas about three months at the time of his death, having landed in North Africa the latter part of July. (*Forest City Courier*, May 18, 1944)

Materials Courtesy of Mrs. Ruth White, <u>Daily Courier</u>, Forest City, North Carolina, and James R. Brown, Publisher

JONES, MARION MCALISTER (MAX)
November 24, 1942

Lieutenant Marion McAlister Jones, youngest son of the Reverend and Mrs. O. G. Jones of Forest City, was killed in the North African area on November 24, 1942. He had just been promoted to First Lieutenant in the Air Corps. Lieutenant Jones, aged 24, was a graduate of the Presbyterian College in Clinton, South Carolina, Class of 1937. He (1918-1942) entered the U.S. Army Air Corps shortly after the outbreak of the war. (*Forest City Courier*, December 16, 1943)

Telegrams received by friends of the Reverend and Mrs. O. J. Jones announced the death of the Joneses' youngest son, Max, Second Lieutenant in the U.S. Army Air Corps. He was killed in action in Northwest Africa, November 24, 1942.

Second Lieutenant Jones was attached to an Army ground aircrew. It was supposed a German bomb killed him during recent strafings somewhere in the neighborhood of Tunisia.

Second Lieutenant Jones, with his parents, made his home in Forest City for a number of years; Dr. Jones was a pastor of the First Presbyterian Church. Dr. Jones retired from active ministry in January of 1942; he and Mrs. Jones had been residing in Pontotoc, Mississippi. (*Rutherford County News*, December 3, 1942)

JORDEN, RALPH R.
1945

Ralph R. Jorden (1923-1945) of Rutherford County gave his life during World War II. Jorden served in the U.S. Army. *(Nancy Stallcup's Honor Roll)*

KIRBY, BOBO VERNER
December 6, 1944

Private Bobo Verner Kirby, of the Prospect Community of Rutherford County, Gaffney, Route 3, was killed in action in France on December 6, 1944. He was reported as missing on November 13.

Private Kirby entered the U.S. Army on March 13, 1944, and took his training at Camp Wheeler, Georgia, and Fort Meade, Maryland. He had been overseas three months. He attended Cliffside High School.

Private Kirby (May 20, 1924-December 6, 1944) was survived by his parents, Mr. and Mrs. J. L. Kirby of near Cliffside; his wife, Grace Jones Kirby; five sisters: Mrs. L. V. McCraw, Mrs. Lindon Spake, and Virginia Kirby, all of Gaffney, Route 3; Mrs. W. F. Huskey, Ellenboro; and Mrs. Guy Hammett, of Chesnee; and four brothers: J. L. Kirby, Jr., Forest City; James Kirby of Gaffney, Route 3; and Corporal Arthur Kirby, U.S. Army, overseas at the time. (*Forest City Courier*, December 28, 1944)

Photo courtesy of Mrs. W. F. Huskey and Mrs. Virginia Scruggs

KIRBY, JAMES W.
March 1, 1945

James W. Kirby, of Rutherfordton, was killed in action in France on March 1, according to a message received by his parents, Mr. and Mrs. K. C. Kirby, of Railroad Avenue, Rutherfordton. He entered service in September and went overseas recently. He landed in France on February 17. He was killed two weeks after entering action. His parents, his wife, and two small children survived him. (*Forest City Courier*, March 22, 1945)

Private James W. Kirby, 21, son of Mrs. K. C. Kirby of Ruth, was killed in action in March in Germany. He entered the U.S. Army on July 12, 1944, and went overseas in February of 1945. He was survived by his mother; one brother: K. C. Kirby, Jr., of Spindale; and six sisters. The six sisters were Mrs. Arlene Gibson, Rutherfordton; Mrs. Roland Wright, Shelby; Mrs. Charles Morrow, Rutherfordton, Route 1; Mrs. Tom Hill and Misses Beatrice and Nell Kirby of Rutherfordton.

Private Kirby (September 29, 1923-March 1, 1945) was a member of an Infantry Battalion of the U.S. Army. In a letter from his commanding officer, he says:

> Your son joined our company 19 February, 1945, and per-formed his duties excellently while with the company. His record was perfect and he was well liked amongst us. All I can inform you of his death is that he was killed instantly in the line of duty and he felt no pain at the time of his death. (*Forest City Courier*, May 3, 1945)

Private Kirby's marker is in the Mt. Pleasant Baptist Cemetery at Sandy Mush. (http://rfci.net/wdfloyd/)

Photo courtesy of <u>Daily Courier</u>, Forest City, North Carolina, and James R. Brown, Publisher

LAVENDER, ARTHUR L.
December 6, 1944

Spindale Soldiers, Brothers Were in Service.

Private First Class Walter S. Lavender, son of Mrs. Nancy E. Lavender of Spindale, enlisted in the U.S. Army August 14, 1940. He took his basic training at Fort Bragg and Camp Shelby, Mississippi. He was stationed at Shreveport, Louisiana. Before enlisting, Private First Class Lavender was an employee of the Stonecutter Mills.

Private William Albert Lavender was inducted into the U.S. Army on September 16, 1942, and received his basic training at Fort Eustis, Virginia. He served overseas. He was employed in Spindale before entering the U.S. Army.

Private Arthur L. Lavender served his country overseas. He entered the Marines on March 7, 1943, and took his training at Parris Island, South Carolina, and New River, North Carolina. Arthur was a brother of Walter and William. All three had a furlough home this year. (*Rutherford County News*, November 11, 1943)

Mrs. Nancy E. Lavender of Spindale received a wire Tuesday inform- ing her of the death of her son Private First Class Arthur Lavender. The wire stated he died of wounds received in action in the South Pacific. He was in the U.S. Marines. He had been in service fifteen months and over- seas ten months. He formerly worked in the Stonecutter Garage, Spindale. He was survived by his mother; two sisters: Mrs. Lee Reid, Lenoir and Miss Nellie Lavender at home; six brothers: Thomas, James, Willis and Lewis Lavender, Spindale; Private First Class William A. Lavender, New Caledonia; Private First Class Walter G. Lavender, Fort Dix, N. J. (*Rutherford County News*, August 17, 1944)

Mrs. Nancy E. Lavender of Spindale was notified of the death of her son Private First Class Arthur Lavender, who died of wounds sustained in action in the South Pacific area. A member of the U.S. Marines Corps, Private First Class Lavender (1922-1944) had been in service fifteen months and overseas ten months. Prior to entering the Marine Corps, he was employed by the Stonecutter Mill at Spindale.

He was survived by his mother; six brothers: Thomas, James, Willis and Lewis Lavender, Spindale; Private First Class William A. Lavender, New Caledonia; Private First Class Walter G. Lavender, Fort Dix, N. J.; and two sisters: Mrs. Lee Reid of Lenoir and Miss Nellie Lavender of Spindale. (*Forest City Courier*, August 24, 1944)

Photo courtesy of <u>*Daily Courier*</u>*, Forest City, North Carolina, and James R. Brown, Publisher*

LOVELACE, ERNEST
December 15, 1943

Private First Class Ernest Lovelace, 22-year-old son of Mr. and Mrs. W. S. Lovelace of the Mooresboro section, was killed in action in Italy on December 15; his parents learned this on Thursday of last week when they received the following telegram:

> The Secretary of War desires me to express his deep regret that your son Private First Class Ernest Lovelace was killed in action in defense of his country on December 15 in Italy. Letter follows. (Signed) Ulio, the Adjutant General.

Private First Class Lovelace (1921-1942) was a former employee of Beacon Manufacturing Company, of Swannanoa. He was called for selective service on August 10, 1942, and received his basic training at Camp Roberts, California. He was then sent to a training camp in New York State for a 30-day period, after which he reported for training at Camp Pickett, Virginia, before being sent overseas in May of 1943. He was a member of Race Path Baptist Church and was well-known in Forest City.

In addition to his parents, he was survived by three brothers: Emmett and Evans Lovelace, the latter a twin, and Yates Lovelace, who was serving with the U.S. Army at Camp Hulen, Texas. He left one sister, Mrs. Mildred Jackson, of this section.

His mother received two letters dated December 12 and 14 on the same day the notification of his death was received. His brother Emmett received a letter dated December 13 from him on the previous day; he said he had received Christmas packages from home and ventured the wish that the homefolks would have an enjoyable holiday. (*Forest City Courier*, January 13, 1944; *Rutherford County News*, August 24, 1944)

LOWERY, LAWSON B.
February 16, 1942

Private Lawson B. Lowery, 23, of near Harris, died in the U.S. Hospital at Oteen February 16, 1942. He was a son of Mrs. Pearly Hayes of Spartanburg, South Carolina, R.F.D. 3. Private Lowery (June 30, 1920-February 16, 1942) was a member of the 99 Quartermaster Corps of the U.S. Army at the time of his death. (*Forest City Courier*, December 16, 1943) He is buried in the Holly Springs Baptist Cemetery. (http://rfci.net/wdfloyd/)

LOWERY, VERNON JOSEPH
January 28, 1943

Private Vernon Joseph Lowery (June 9, 1921-January 28, 1943) of Henrietta was killed in action in the Pacific area combat zone on January 28, 1943; the parents, Mr. and Mrs. Vernon J. Lowery, Sr., did not receive word of his death until nearly a month later. He had been in the U.S. Army one year. (*Forest City Courier*, Big Issue, August 12, 1943; Photo: *Forest City Courier*, December 16, 1943) He is buried in the Holly Springs Baptist Cemetery. (http://rfci.net/wdfloyd/)

Photo courtesy of <u>Daily Courier</u>, Forest City, North Carolina, and James R. Brown, Publisher

MASON, DANIEL DEWITT
September 21, 1945

Daniel Dewitt Mason, Pharmacist Mate Second Class, U.S. Navy, was killed in an accident at a South Pacific base on September 21, according to a message received by his wife, Mrs. Ernestine Mason of Henrietta.

According to the meager details available, Pharmacist Mate Second Class Mason (July 21, 1923-September 21, 1945) was accidentally killed in an accident involving a truck and a tractor at Base Hospital No. 4, Navy 3256, in the South Pacific area.

He was a son of Mr. and Mrs. Daniel H. Mason of Henrietta. (*Rutherford County News*, October 25, 1945) He is buried in the High Shoal Baptist Cemetery. (http://rfci.net/wdfloyd/)

Daniel Dewitt Mason is the next-to-the-last person on the front row in front of Henrietta Elementary School. The back row includes Faye Estep, James Green, Jack Goode, J. W. Waters, Max Hicks. The next-to-the back row includes ___ Nodine, ____, Lillie McSwain, Vera Jane Wall, ____, Floyd Heckerd, L. C. Wall. The first row includes Margaret McDaniel, Louise Clayton, Lyles Mason, Ralph Clayton, ____, Eve Watts, Daniel DeWitt Mason, and Charlie Newton.

Photography courtesy of Lyles Mason

MATHENY, CLYDE MARVIN
May 14, 1945

Three Rutherford County men have been reported killed in action this week, to bring Rutherford County's total casualty list to 111 dead and 20 missing.

Private First Class Clyde Matheny, 22, U.S. Marine Corps, was killed in action on Okinawa on May 14th, according to a message received here today by his wife, Mrs. Jeannette Kiser Matheny of the Bostic Road, Forest City. (*Forest City Courier*, May 24, 1945) Private Matheny was killed at Sugar Loaf Hill in Okinawa. *(Fred Matheny)*

Private Matheny (May 27, 1923- May 14, 1945) entered service two years ago and had been overseas about a year. He was survived by his wife; his mother, Mrs. Esther Bailey Matheny (Mrs. Forest Timmons Matheny) of Ellenboro; a son, Forest; four brothers: Fred Matheny in the U.S. Army, Max, Vernon, and Harry Matheny of Ellenboro; three sisters: Mrs. Robert Jackson of Rock Hill, Louise, and Irene of Ellenboro. (*Forest City Courier*, May 24, 1945)

He is buried in the Racepath Baptist Church Cemetery, Ellenboro. (http://rfci.net/wdfloyd/)

Forest Matheny, Private First Class Clyde Matheny's son, was the head mechanic on the plane of President Richard Nixon. *(Fred Matheny)*

Photo courtesy of Daily Courier, Forest City, North Carolina, and James R. Brown, Publisher

*Photos courtesy of
Fred Matheny*

MATHIS, RALPH NESBURT
October 6, 1944

Private First Class Ralph Nesburt Mathis, aged 22, of Rutherfordton, was killed in action in France on October 6, according to a message received by his parents, Mr. and Mrs. Elam Mathis of Rutherfordton, Route 2.

Private First Class Mathis (September 27, 1922-October 6, 1944) of the U.S. Army was survived by his parents; five sisters: Mrs. Janie Price, Mrs. Sallie Beheler, Virginia, Rebecca, and Mary Mathis; and one brother, Sherrill Mathis. Private First Class Mathis was first reported as missing in action. (*Forest City Courier*, November 30, 1944) He is buried in the Lum Green River Baptist Church Cemetery, Polk County. (http://rfci.net/wdfloyd/)

MAXWELL, JEROME WILLIAM
April 16, 1945

Jerome William Maxwell, Chief Electrician's Mate, U.S. Navy, aged 24, of Rutherfordton, was killed in action in the Pacific Theatre of War, according to a message received by his parents, Mr. and Mrs. W. R. Maxwell of Rutherfordton, Route 2.

His death brought Rutherford County's total casualty list to 113 men dead in World War II.

Chief Petty Officer (Electrician's Mate, U.S. Navy) Maxwell (born October 5, 1920) entered the Navy in March of 1942 and was sent on sea duty in August of 1942. He spent 25 months in England, North Africa, and in the invasion of Sicily. He was returned to the States last September, and after a furlough at home left for Pacific duty in December of 1944.

He was buried in an allied cemetery on a South Pacific Island.

Chief Maxwell was survived by his parents; his widow, Mrs. Lena Lipe Maxwell, formerly of Charlotte and daughter of Mr. and Mrs. C. H. Lipe of Mount Pleasant; and the following brothers and sisters: Miss Frances Maxwell of Spindale, Private Carey P. Maxwell, in Germany; Wilton Maxwell, Jr.; Hall Maxwell; Charles Maxwell; and Misses Wiletta, Shirley Ann, Ramona Lou, and Carolyn Maxwell at home. (*Forest City Courier,* June 7, 1945)

Prior to joining the U.S. Navy in March of 1942, Chief Petty Officer Maxwell was employed by the Electric Service Company at Hickory.

Mrs. Maxwell, whom he married on October 11, 1941, had been living with her parents at Mount Pleasant. She took a job in Charlotte and was working in 1945 for a mutual insurance company. *(Information courtesy of Ruth Maxwell)*

He is now buried in the Oak Springs Baptist Cemetery. (http://rfci.net/wdfloyd/)

Photos courtesy of Ruth Maxwell

MCAFEE, DONALD W.

Sergeant Donald W. McAfee of the U.S. Army and of Rutherford County was killed in service of his country during World War II.

(Nancy Stallcup's Memorial Garden Honor List)

McCURRY, PRESTON N.
May 31, 1944

Sergeant Preston N. McCurry, 21, son of Mr. and Mrs. A. C. McCurry of Bostic, Route 2, was killed in action in Italy on May 31, according to a War Department announcement received Monday by his parents.

Sergeant McCurry was born February 19, 1923. The Cramerton Mills of Cramerton employed him before he entered the U.S. Army on December 12, 1942, at Camp Phillips, Kansas. He trained later at Camp Forrest, Tennessee, and Fort Meade, Maryland. He landed in North Africa on November 15, 1943, and went to Italy from that point.

Sergeant McCurry, a member of the U.S. Army Infantry Regiment, was married to Miss Sarah Love, June 30, 1942. He was a nephew of Messrs. P. N. and T. T. Long of Forest City. (*Forest City Courier*, July 6, 1944) He is buried in the Mt. Harmony Baptist Cemetery. (http://rfci.net/wdfloyd/)

Photo courtesy of Daily Courier, Forest City, North Carolina, and James R. Brown, Publisher

MCDANIEL, THERON A.
April 12, 1945

Sergeant Theron McDaniel, 20, of Spindale, was killed in action in the South Pacific on April 12, 1945, according to a message received last week. He entered service about a year ago and had been overseas about six months. (*Forest City Courier*, May 10, 1945)

Sergeant McDaniel was a son of Mr. and Mrs. R. A. McDaniel of Cliffside. Sergeant McDaniel had been stationed in Pennsylvania when he was stateside. (*Forest City Courier*, Big Issue, August 12, 1943)

Photo courtesy of Daily Courier, Forest City, North Carolina, and James R. Brown, Publisher

McDaniel, Theron E.
April 22, 1945

A special memorial service was held for Private First Class Theron E. McDaniel of Spindale on Sunday, July 29, 1945, at 3:00 p.m. The service was in the Spencer Baptist Church of Spindale. The pastor, the Reverend C. C. Matheny, read the Scriptures. Reverend J. A. Brock of Shelby, former pastor, delivered the memorial address. A quartet composed of Dr. W. L. Stallings, W. C. Grayson, W. H. Fagan, and Frank Smith, all of Forest City, sang "Crossing the Bar" and "Abide With Me."

The Reverend Olen Kendrick pronounced the benediction; D. C. Cole blew Taps.

Private First Class McDaniel was the son of the late Mr. and Mrs. E. L. McDaniel of Spindale and the husband of Mrs. Margaret Higgins McDaniel of Higgins, Yancey County. He was born at Gilkey on February 3, 1916. He joined the Spencer Baptist Church at 20. He entered the service on November 2, 1943, and served overseas 11 months in New Guinea, the Netherlands, the East Indies, and Luzon, Philippines.

He died on Luzon on April 22, 1945. (*Forest City Courier*, July 26, 1945)

MCFARLAND, JOHN F.

Private First Class John F. McFarland of the U.S. Army and of Rutherford County was killed in service of his country during World War II.

(Nancy Stallcup's Memorial Garden Honor List)

MCGINNIS, BILLY
March 1942

Billy McGinnis, Seaman First Class of the U.S. Navy, was reported killed in action in a naval engagement in March of 1942. No details of his death were given out by the Navy Department. He went down with his ship.

He enlisted in the Navy while residing with his parents, Mr. and Mrs. G. M. McGinnis, at Chimney Rock. The parents reside in Asheville. (*Forest City Courier*, Big Issue, August 12, 1943)

MCKEITHAN, LEWIS W.
April 16, 1944

Word was received here that Private Lewis McKeithan of Bostic died in Chunking, China, April 16 of injuries received last October.

The death of Private McKeithan brought Rutherford County's casualty list for World War II to 30 men dead and five unaccounted for and missing.

Private McKeithan, aged 40, a son of the late Mr. and Mrs. Dan McKeithan of Bostic, had been in the U.S. Army for some time; he was stationed with the American Air Forces in China as photographer and aerial gunner.

Private McKeithan (February 17, 1904-April 16, 1944) was survived by the following brothers and sisters: Mrs. Burwell Moore, Forest City; Mrs. Buena Ferree and Mrs. Boyd Higgins, Bostic; Mrs. Walter Settlemyre, Alexander Mill; Mrs. Charles Laughridge, Rocky Mount; Mrs. Bessie Howell. The brothers were Tim McKeithan, Bostic; Frank McKeithan, Wilmington; Dick McKeithan, with the U.S. Army in England; and Marsh McKeithan of Georgia.

Prior to entering the U.S. Army, Private McKeithan was an interior decorator. (*Forest City Courier*, May 4, 1944) He is buried in the Concord Baptist Church Cemetery. (http://rfci.net/wdfloyd/)

Photo courtesy of Daily Courier, *Forest City, North Carolina, and James R. Brown, Publisher*

McKINNEY, BROADUS H.
December 11, 1944

Three were dead and eight wounded to bring Rutherford County's casualty list of World War II to eleven for the week. The dead were Private First Class Broadus H. McKinney, Private Earl McKinney, and Private First Class Arnold B. Crotts.

Private First Class Broadus H. McKinney (1922-1944) of Green Hill, Rutherfordton Star Route, was killed in action December 11 in Burma, according to a message received last week by his father, Joseph A. McKinney also of Green Hill. Private First Class McKinney was with the U.S. Army.

This was the second son of this family to be killed in action in World War II. An older brother, Private Earl McKinney, was killed September 22, 1944, in Germany. There was only one other instance of two Rutherford brothers being killed in action in this war. The other two brothers killed were Private First Class Toy Ruppe and Private First Class Lynn Ruppe, both of Cliffside.

Private First Class McKinney entered the U.S. Army in February of 1943 and went overseas in May of 1944. He was survived by his parents and five brothers, four of whom were in service: one in Hawaii, one in China, one in the Philippines, and one in a camp in Alabama. (*Forest City Courier*, January 4, 1945)

MCKINNEY, R. EARL
September 22, 1944

Three were dead and eight wounded on January 4, 1945, to bring Rutherford County's casualty list of World War II to eleven for the week. The dead were Private First Class Broadus H. McKinney, Private Earl McKinney, and Private First Class Arnold B. Crotts.

Private R. Earl McKinney, the older brother of the two, was killed September 22, 1944, in Germany. There was only one other instance of two Rutherford brothers being killed in action in this war. The other two brothers killed were Private First Class Toy Ruppe and Private First Class Lynn Ruppe, both of Cliffside.

The younger brother Private First Class Broadus H. McKinney of Green Hill, Rutherfordton Star Route, was killed in action December 11 in Burma, according to a message received last week by his father, Joseph A. McKinney also of Green Hill.

Private McKinney (1908-1944) was survived by his parents and six brothers, five of whom were in service: one in Hawaii, one in China, one in the Philippines, one in Burma, and one in a camp in Alabama. (*Forest City Courier*, January 4, 1945)

MILLER, PHILIP
October 21, 1942

In making a check of Rutherford County's World War II dead, it was learned that Private Philip Miller, aged 25, Rutherfordton resident, was killed in Venice, Florida, in an accident on October 21, 1942. Miller (October 12, 1919-October 21, 1942) was a member of the U.S. Army Tank Corps and had enlisted from Port Washington, New York. His body was brought to Rutherfordton for burial. He was a son of Mrs. Eliza Miller of Rutherfordton. (*Forest City Courier*, October 25, 1945) He is buried in the New Hope Cemetery. (http://rfci.net/wdfloyd/)

MILLER, WALTER C.
December 3, 1944

The War Department informed Mrs. Ollie J. Miller of Forest City that her son Second Lieutenant Walter C. Miller (1918-1944) was presumed to be dead. Twelve months have expired without receipt of evidence to support a continued presumption of survival.

Lieutenant Miller's death brought Rutherford County's World War II casualty list to 127 dead and three still missing.

The message to Mrs. Miller read:

> Since your son, Second Lieutenant Walter C. Miller, Air Corps, was reported missing in action December 1944, the War Department has entertained the hope that he survived and that information would be revealed dispelling the uncertainty surrounding his absence.
>
> However, as in many cases, the conditions of warfare deny us such information. The record concerning your son shows that he was a crewmember aboard a B-29 Superfortress aircraft and that he failed to return from a bombing mission in Tokyo, Japan. This plane was damaged by enemy aircraft over the target and was ditched at 3:15 p.m. at some unidentified point between Tokyo and its base on Saipan, Marianas Islands, while returning to the latter. An exhaustive search was made by Army and Navy planes and Navy surface vessels, but at the end of a month no one had been found.

Lieutenant Miller entered the U.S. Army Air Forces in January of 1942 and went overseas in September of 1944 as a bombardier. Prior to entering service he was a teller at the Union Trust Company. He was survived by his mother, Mrs. Ollie Miller of Forest City; three brothers, Private First Class Charles Roger Miller, Forest City, a former prisoner of war of the German Government; Ernest Miller, Asheville; G. B. Miller of Forest City, and one sister, Mrs. Paul Daniel, of Forest City. (*Forest City Courier*, December 13, 1945)

Belle Daniel, Lieutenant Miller's sister, has a later handwritten note that came to her mother and is now in her possession. The note reads:

Additional information has been received indicating that Lt. Miller was a crew member of a B-29 which departed from Saipan on a bombing mission to Tokyo Japan on December 3, 1944. The report reveals that during this mission enroute from the target our planes encountered hostile aircraft and in the ensuing engagement your son's bomber sustained damage and subsequently crash landed at about 3:15 p.m. near Hachijo Jima Island.

Photos courtesy of Mrs. Paul Daniel and Daily Courier, Forest City, North Carolina, and James R. Brown, Publisher

MOREHEAD, FRANK BROWNING
October 4, 1944

Private Frank Browning Morehead of Avondale was killed in action in Italy on October 4, according to a message received by his wife, the former Frances Harrill of Forest City; her parents were Mr. and Mrs. J. K. Harrill of Forest City.

Private Morehead (May 25, 1916-October 4, 1944), who was attached to an Infantry Regiment in the medical detachment, entered the U. S. Army on September 17, 1943. Prior to that he was engaged as a pharmacist at Mooneyham Drug Store in Avondale.

His wife, who was assistant postmaster at Avondale, and his parents, Mr. and Mrs. Bate Morehead of Henrietta and Avondale, survived him. He was a member of the Avondale Methodist Church. (*Forest City Courier*, November 9, 1944)

Mrs. Frank B. Morehead was presented the Silver Star Medal at Camp Croft, South Carolina, April 14th. The Silver Star was awarded her husband, the late Frank B. Morehead, posthumously for gallantry in action, October 4th, 1944, in Italy.

When the platoon in which he was attached as medical aid man was attacking an enemy-held hill under withering machine gun and sniper fire, several of the platoon were wounded but managed to reach a place of safety. Seeing one soldier seriously wounded and lying in the line of enemy fire, Private Morehead, completely aware of the danger in attempting to rescue and disregarding the warning of others nearby, rushed to the aid of the wounded man.

Although under direct enemy observation, he administered first aid; while evacuating his comrade, he was seriously wounded by enemy fire. Disregarding his own wounds, which later proved fatal, he persisted in evacuating the casualty to a place of safety. His outstanding courage and self-sacrifice saved the wounded man's life and reflect the highest traditions of the military service. (*Forest City Courie*r, April 28, 1945) He is buried in the Sharon Methodist Cemetery, Cleveland County. (http://rfci.net/wdfloyd/)

MORGAN, FRED OWENSBY
October 26, 1942

Mr. and Mrs. Lawrence O. Morgan of near town had the following wire from the Navy Department Friday:

> The Navy Department deeply regrets to inform you that your son Fred Owensby Morgan, Machinists Mate, Second Class, USN, was missing following action in the performance of his duty and in the service of his country. The Department appreciates your great anxiety but details are not available and delay in receipt thereof must necessarily be expected to prevent possible aid to our enemies. Rear Admiral Randall Jacobs, Chief of Naval Personnel.

It was thought that young Morgan of the U.S. Navy was in the Guadalcanal battle. He had been in the Navy three years. He finished at Central High in 1938. He was at home Christmas 1940. He had been in the Pacific for the past year and was at Pearl Harbor on December 7.

Mr. and Mrs. Morgan have another son, Worth G. Morgan, who was in the Philadelphia Navy Yard awaiting his new ship the *Santa Fe*, a large new cruiser. (*Rutherfordton News*, November 19, 1942)

Subsequent article . . .

Mr. and Mrs. Lawrence Morgan of near town have received a Purple Heart, awarded to their deceased son. Fred O. Morgan (1919-1942) was killed October 26, 1942 in the Pacific. The Purple Heart came in a case and gave his rating, etc. (*Forest City Courier*, August 2, 1945)

Fred O. Morgan was on the U.S.S. *Hornet* (CV8). The ship was sunk after being damaged by aircraft torpedoes at the Battle of Santa Cruz, October 26, 1942. The planes that bombed Tokyo in April of 1942 came from the U.S.S. *Hornet*; the ship was high on the list of targets to be destroyed because of its role in the bombing of Tokyo. Fred O. Morgan, Machinists Mate, Second Class, USN, was in the boiler room when the ship sank, according to his brother Worth Morgan.

Worth Morgan, his brother, was on an escort ship, the U.S. *Vincennes* (CA44), a heavy cruiser, at the time of the death of Fred Owensby Morgan, Machinists Mate, Second Class, USN. (Information from Worth Griffin Morgan)

Photo on previous page courtesy of <u>Daily Courier</u>, Forest City, North Carolina, and James R. Brown, Publisher

Worth Morgan is the figure with the hat (on the left).
Fred Owensby Morgan is the figure on the right.

Photo courtesy of Worth Morgan

MORGAN, OTIS F.
December 15, 1944

First Lieutenant Otis F. Morgan, of Spindale, taken prisoner by the Japanese when Corrigidor fell in early 1942, was killed on December 15, 1944; as a member of the U.S. Navy, he was aboard a Japanese transport ship and was presumably headed for the Japanese Islands. His mother, Mrs. Lissie Morgan of Spindale and Wilmington, Delaware, received a letter from the War Department.

> From the available information, it appears that 1,619 prisoners of war were embarked December 13, 1944, at Manila, on a Japanese vessel presumably for transfer to Japan. The ship was bombed and sunk in Subic Bay, Luzon, Philippine Islands, December 15, 1944. After considerable delay there has been received from the Japanese government a confirmatory report of this sinking, with partial official list of those lost and of the survivors. Nine hundred and forty-two of the prisoners of war, among them your son, are officially reported by the Japanese to have lost their lives at the time.

Lieutenant Morgan was survived by his mother; a brother, Hugh Morgan of Laurens, South Carolina; a sister: Mrs. J. R. Logan of Bishopville, South Carolina; and several uncles and aunts, including W. R. Morgan, Mrs. W. C. Montfredo, L. T. Rollins, and Mrs. Susie Harper, all of Spindale.

Lieutenant Morgan attended Laurens, South Carolina High School, graduated from Clemson College, and was residing in Aiken, South Carolina, when he entered service in the Reserve Officers Corps in 1941.

Lieutenant Morgan's death brought Rutherford County's total World War II dead to 118 men. (*Forest City Courier*, August 2, 1945)

MORRIS, JOHN A.
July 29, 1944

World War II continues to exact a toll of Rutherford County men killed, wounded, and missing. The total dead from the county was 53 as of August 24, 1944.

Private John A. Morris, 27, was killed in action in France on July 29. On August 11 a letter from his wife was returned marked "deceased" by a Lieutenant who was a special friend of John.

Private Morris had been overseas about four months and in the U.S. Army a year; he was in the infantry. He married Frances Moore of Forest City four years ago. His widow; his father, R. E. Morris; and a sister, Mrs. Dewey Carpenter of the Mt. Vernon section survived him. Another sister also survived; she was Lieutenant Evelyn Morris, a nurse in Rome, Italy. He also had three brothers, Ovid Morris, teacher at Beth-Ware school near Kings Mountain; G. Arnold Morris, Salisbury; and Robert Morris, Savannah, Georgia.

A short memorial service will be held at Brittain Presbyterian Church, Sunday, August 27 at 3:30 p.m. in honor of John Morris (1917-1944). He was a loyal member of this church. (*Rutherford County News*, August 24, 1944)

Rutherford County's casualty list for the week shows three dead, five wounded, two missing, and one a prisoner of war; this was a total of 11 casualties. This was a decided slump in the number of casualties reported in any one week since the invasion of France.

Private First Class John A. Morris, aged 27, was killed in action July 29 in France, according to a message received by his wife, Mrs. Frances Moore Morris of Forest City, Sunday. Private First Class Morris, son of R. E. Morris and the late Mrs. Morris of Forest City, Route 2 entered service August 9, 1943, and went overseas in April of 1944, as a member of an Infantry Regiment.

He was survived by his wife, his father, and the following brothers and sisters: O. W. Morris, Kings Mountain; Robert E. Morris, Jr., Savannah, Georgia; Arnold Morris, Salisbury; Lieutenant Evelyn Morris, U.S. Army Nurse Corps, now in Italy; and Mrs. Dewey Carpenter of Forest City, Route 2. Young Morris graduated from Mt. Vernon High School in the class of 1937. He was married four years before his death. He was 27 years of age at the time of his death. (*Forest City Courier*, August 24, 1944)

Photos courtesy of
Mrs. Walda Carpenter

MORROW, MARVIN D.
November 17, 1944

Private First Class Marvin D. Morrow, son of Mr. and Mrs. O. T. Morrow of Forest City, Route 2, was killed in action in Germany on November 17, 1944, according to a telegram received by his family last week. Private First Class Morrow (1922-1944) entered the U.S. Army on December 27, 1942, took his basic training at Fort McClellan, Alabama, and went overseas in May 1943. He was attached to the infantry of the First Army, which was the first to land in Africa, Sicily, and France; the first to break out of the Normandy Beachhead; and the first to force the Siegfried Line.

His parents and five brothers, three of whom were overseas and one of whom was given a medical discharge following foreign service, survived Private First Class Morrow. Private Thomas E. and Clarence E. were in France; John Cecil was in New Guinea; Taylor had recently returned from overseas; and Walter was in the home.

Private First Class Morrow was educated at Harris High School and at the time of his enlistment was employed by Florence Mills. He was 22 years old. (*Forest City Courier*, December 14, 1944)

Photo courtesy of Janet Carpenter

Additional article:

Colonel Wilbur J. Fox of Camp Croft, South Carolina, presented Mr. and Mrs. O. T. Morrow of Forest City, Route 2, the Bronze Star Medal with Oak Leaf Cluster awarded to their son Private First Class Marvin D. Morrow. The ceremony was on Sunday afternoon at 2:00 o'clock at their home.

Private First Class Morrow received the Bronze Star Medal for heroic achievement on August 3, 1943, and the Oak Leaf Cluster for heroic achievement on June 6, 1944, on the First Army fronts. He was attached to the Infantry with the 85th Division. Private First Class Morrow was killed in action on November 17, 1944. (*Forest City Courier*, August 16, 1945)

Three Forest City Soldiers

Pfc. Taylor Morrow   *Pvt. Marvin D. Morrow*   *John C. Morrow*

Photos courtesy of <u>Daily Courier</u>, Forest City, North Carolina, and James R. Brown, Publisher

MOSS, RAY
May 2, 1945

Corporal Ray Moss of Spindale was killed in action in Germany on May 2, 1945, according to a message received Saturday by his wife, Mrs. Imogene Yelton Moss of Spindale.

Corporal Moss was 28 years of age. He entered the U.S. Army in May of 1942 and had been overseas since May of 1943. He was a member of a Paratrooper Division of the U.S. Army Air Corps. Prior to entering service he was employed in the weave room at Stonecutter Mill.

Corporal Moss (1915?-1945) was survived by his wife; two children: Patricia and Lee, who make their home in Spindale; and two sisters, Mrs. Marock Smith and Mrs. Clarence Taylor, both of Spindale. (*Forest City Courier*, May 24, 1945)

Corporal Ray Moss enlisted in the Paratroopers of the Army Air Corps on June 17, 1942, and took his basic training at Camp Wheeler, Georgia, and later he qualified as a Paratrooper with five jumps. On November 14 of last year he was sent to Fort Bragg for further training. In April of 1943, he landed in North Africa for active duty. In civilian life he held a position with the Stonecutter Mills Company. His wife and two children reside in Spindale. (*Forest City Courier*, May 31, 1945)

Photo courtesy of Daily Courier, Forest City, North Carolina, and James R. Brown, Publisher

MULL, HARRISON B.
May 25, 1945

Sergeant Harrison B. Mull was killed on May 25, 1945, in Okinawa by a Japanese sniper. Sergeant Mull's immediate supervisor had been killed, and Sergeant Mull was acting Lieutenant when he was attacked. After he was wounded twice, he killed three of the enemy before he was hit in the heart by the sniper.

Sergeant Harrison B. Mull was born November 20, 1915, in Rutherfordton, North Carolina; his parents were George and Mary Early Mull. On April 16, 1937, he married Ruby Ricker Mull in Murphy, North Carolina. They had four children: Barbara Imogene Mull (Divido), born February 1, 1938; Carl Ray Mull, born January 7, 1941; Opal Carolyn Mull (Dooly), born April 2, 1943; and Betty Joan Mull (Cornelius), born April 10, 1945.

Sergeant Mull was a kind and gentle man loved by all who knew him. He could have avoided the Armed Services because he had three children and he was colorblind. He felt it was his duty to fight alongside his brother and all the other brave men who fought for our nation. He made the ultimate sacrifice.

Sergeant Harrison B. Mull is buried in the Bill's Creek Baptist Church Cemetery, 1469 Bill's Creek Road, Lake Lure, North Carolina. 28746 (Contributed by Virginia D. Wilson, 1364 Bill's Creek Road, Lake Lure, North Carolina 28746)

Photo courtesy of Virginia D. Wilson

NANNEY, CHARLES EDWARD
August 9, 1945

Rejoicing over peace in the home of Mr. and Mrs. Addie D. Nanney, South Broadway, Forest City, was cut short Wednesday morning upon receipt of a telegram from the Navy Department. The telegram informed them that their son Charles Edward Nanny, 19, had been killed in action.

Charles Edward Nanney, Gunners Mate Third Class, U.S. Navy, was killed in action last Thursday in the South Pacific area.

Gunners Mate Third Class Charles Nanney (June 22, 1926-August 9, 1945) graduated from

Forest City High School in the Class of 1943. He entered a Naval V-12 Class in November of that year. Later he withdrew from the class and entered the regular Navy.

He was survived by his parents, Mr. and Mrs. Nanney; and three brothers: Allen D. Nanney, Charlotte; and Bobby and Don Nanney at home. (*Forest City Courier*, August 16, 1945)

His death was five days before the end of the war. At that time 11 sailors, six marines and 102 soldiers from Rutherford County had died during the war period. (*Forest City Courier*, August 23, 1945)

The Navy Department posthumously awarded the Purple Heart to Charles Nanney, Gunners Mate, Third Class, U.S. Navy, who was killed in action last August. His parents, Mr. and Mrs. A. D. Nanney of Forest City, received the medal this week. (*Forest City Courier*, February 28, 1946)

Charles E. Nanney, Gunners Mate Third Class, U.S. Navy, was in the Class of 1932; he entered a Naval V-12 Class in November of 1943. Later he withdrew from the class and entered the regular Navy.

His parents and three brothers—Allen D. Nanney of Charlotte; Bobby and Don Nanney of the home—survived the nineteen-year-old. (*Forest City Courier*, September 13, 1945) His marker is in the Cool Springs Cemetery, Section #5. (http://rfci.net/wdfloyd/)

Photo courtesy of <u>Daily Courier</u>, Forest City, North Carolina, and James R. Brown, Publisher

NEWTON, ROBERT E.
November 9, 1944

Private First Class Robert E. Newton (1919-1944) of Rutherfordton was wounded in the Mediterranean battle area, according to an announcement from the War Department. He was a son of Mrs. Fannie E. Newton of Rutherfordton. He was one of 485 soldiers wounded in action last week. (*Forest City Courier*, January 6, 1944)

Sergeant Robert E. Newton, son of Mr. and Mrs. J. K. Newton of Rutherfordton, was killed in action November 9, 1944, in France. He had been overseas two years and in the U.S. Army for three years. His parents, five brothers, and three sisters survived him. (*Forest City Courier*, December 21, 1944)

OWENS, DAVID MARTIN
July 13, 1944

Private First Class David Martin Owens, son of Mr. and Mrs. Arthur Owens of Rutherfordton, was killed in France on July 13, 1944, according to a wire from Washington to his family. Private First Class Owens (1922-1944) enlisted in the U.S. Army on October 19, 1942, and went overseas in April of 1944. His parents and several brothers and sisters survived him. (*Rutherford County News*, August 10, 1944)

PADGETT, BUFORD H.
August 20, 1943

World War II laid a heavy hand on Rutherford County during the past week, exacting as a toll three dead and four wounded in action. The deaths of these three Rutherford soldiers brought the county's list of World War II dead to 19.

Private First Class Buford H. Padgett (1912-1943) of Mooresboro, Route 1, was killed in the Pacific area. Mr. and Mrs. B. W. Padgett of Mooresboro, Route 1, received notice from the War Department on Thursday afternoon that their son Private First Class Buford H. Padgett of the U.S. Army died in the Pacific area where he was serving with the United States Army on August 20.

The telegram read:

> The Secretary of War asks that I assure you of his deep sympathy in the loss of your son, Private First Class Buford H. Padgett. Report received states that he died August 20 in the Pacific area as the result of an accident. Letter follows.

Private First Class Padgett entered service in August last year and sailed for overseas duty in January. Prior to entering service he was engaged in farming with his father. He was 30 years of age and was the eighteenth death from Rutherford County.

Surviving besides the parents were one brother, Boyd Padgett of the home, and four sisters, Miss Ethel Padgett and Mrs. Dewey Brown of the home; Mrs. Emmitt Hamrick of Ellenboro; and Mrs. Lad Brooks of Mooresboro. (*Forest City Courier*, September 9, 1943)

Photo courtesy of Mrs. Ethel Padgett Tate and Mr. Bobby Joe Hamrick

PARKER, JOHN A.
June 21, 1944

Mr. and Mrs. G. B. Parker of Ruth received a message from the War Department Wednesday that their son, Corporal John A. Parker was missing in action, in the European Theater of War. He had been missing since June 9th. Corporal Parker entered the service in November of 1941 and had been overseas 22 months. (*Forest City Courier*, June 29, 1944)

Reports have been received on two Rutherford County war casualties this week: Private Zeb C. Cartee of Rutherfordton, Route 1, and Corporal John A. Parker (May 18, 1918-June 21, 1944) of Rutherfordton; both were killed in action. (*Forest City Courier*, September 7, 1944) Corporal Parker of the U.S. Army is buried in the Rutherfordton City Cemetery, Section #4. (http://rfci.net/wdfloyd/)

POOLE, HERBERT
October 1, 1943

Private First Class Herbert Poole, son of Mrs. Belle Poole and the late John Poole of Forest City died October 1 in Algeria. He entered the U.S. Army on January 28, 1943. Three days preceding his induction to the U.S. Army he was married to Miss Juanita Henson of Forest City. (*Rutherford County News*, November 25, 1943)

Word was received here Thursday morning that Private First Class Herbert Poole, son of Mrs. Belle Poole and the late John Poole of Forest City, died October 1 in Algeria. Herbert, who was well known and very popular among the younger set here, had been overseas only a few weeks. He was 20 years of age. The cause of his death was not revealed in the message from the War Department.

The Forest City youth entered the service January 28, 1943. Three days preceding his induction he was married to Miss Juanita Henson of Forest City. In addition to his wife, he was survived by his mother, Mrs. Bell Poole; two brothers: William, who was in the Merchant Marine, and Tommie at home; and a sister, Mary Francis Poole.

Herbert graduated from Cool Springs High School here and attended Appalachian State Teachers College, Boone. He was a member of the First Baptist Church.

His father, the late John T. Poole, who died in September of 1942, was a prominent Forest City businessman and chief of the Forest City volunteer fire department for 18 years. (*Forest City Courier*, November 11, 1943)

PRICE, ARTHUR F.
December 28, 1944

Corporal Arthur F. Price, aged 20, of Ellenboro, was killed in action in Germany, according to a message received by his parents, Mr. and Mrs. P. R. Price, of Ellenboro.

Corporal Price (1924-1944) had been serving in the U.S. Army since August 1943 and went overseas last September. He was survived by his parents: Plato Rollins Price and Nettie Lee Owensby Price (April 19, 1892-May 15, 1967; Bethel Baptist Church Cemetery, Ellenboro); his widow, Mrs. Nellie D. Price (Nell Price Burns, May 25, 1923 February 3, 1998; Bethel Baptist Church Cemetery, Ellenboro), and a small daughter Anita (March 8, 1943-), who reside with his parents in Ellenboro; a sister, Mrs. Ervin Grindstaff (June 10, 1912-January 10, 1983) of Ellenboro; three brothers: Edward Rollins Price (October 9, 1913-) of Ellenboro; Corporal Falls William Price (July 12, 1918-), serving with the First Army in Belgium; and Sergeant Roy Donald Price (May 11, 1921-May 19, 1982; Bethel Baptist Church Cemetery, Ellenboro) who was wounded in action and was recuperating in a hospital in England. Prior to entering service, Corporal Price was employed by Grindstaff's Store in Ellenboro. He was a graduate of Ellenboro High School. (*Forest City Courier*, January 18, 1945)

At the request of his next of kin, Plato Rollins Price (February 22, 1887-November 4, 1976; Bethel Baptist Church Cemetery, Ellenboro), Route 1, Mooresboro, North Carolina, Corporal Arthur F. Price was brought to the United States aboard the United States Army Transport *Haiti Victory* in 1949. The remains of 91 North Carolinians who lost their lives during World War II were returned at that time. Corporal Price had been originally interred in a temporary military cemetery in Holland. (*Forest City Courier*, March 18, 1949) He is now buried in the National Cemetery in Salisbury, North Carolina.

Photograph in possession of Author, Anita Price Davis (his daughter).

153

PRICE, JOSEPH MADISON, JR.
November 26, 1944

Technical Sergeant Five Joseph Madison Price, U.S. Army Air Forces, who had been reported missing in action in Europe since November 26, 1944, was believed to have been killed on that date. The War Department notified his mother, Mrs. J. M. Price of Forest City, Route 1. Technical Sergeant Five Price (September 24, 1920-November 26, 1944) was a member of a crew of a Flying Fortress, based in England, which was seen to fall during a bombing mission over Germany.

When over Zwalle, Holland, they encountered heavy anti-aircraft fire, and his plane dropped behind the others in formation. His plane was last seen over the Dutch coast. He was a member of the Eighth Air Force and had completed 18 missions. He was survived by his wife, the former Miss Cassie Wagnon of Washington, D.C.; his mother; three brothers: Bruce and Jake Price of Caroleen and John Price, U. S. Navy; and two sisters: Mrs. J. R. McDaniel of Caroleen and Mrs. Max Padgett of Forest City. (*Forest City Courier*, December 6, 1945; *Forest City Courier*, January 25, 1946) He is buried in the Mt. Pleasant Baptist Church Cemetery at Sandy Mush. (http://rfci.net/wdfloyd/)

Photo courtesy of Daily Courier, Forest City, North Carolina, and James R. Brown, Publisher

Joseph Madison Price was an Engineer Gunner on a B-17 Bomber with the 398th Bomber Squadron. In his last letter home, he stated that by the grace of God he had completed 18 missions and after 25 missions he could return home. On his 19th mission his plane was shot down and fell into the North Sea near the Netherlands. He was declared missing in action on November 27, 1944.

In the summer of 1945, a fisherman discovered the bodies of the crew washed ashore in Urk, Holland, He wrote Joe's mother and the parents of the other crewmembers and stated that the bodies had been preserved in the icy waters and that they appeared to have been dead only a few hours.

The bodies of the crew were buried in a church cemetery in Urk, Holland. Later they were placed in a National Cemetery in Belgium. When the cemetery was being disposed of after the war, Joe's body was sent home.

Story and photograph courtesy of Wynelle Price McDaniel.

PRINCE, CHARLES W.
February 1942 (February 28, 1942)

Mr. and Mrs. Clarence Lancaster Prince received the following message from the Navy Department:

> The Navy Department deeply regrets to inform you that your son, Charles William Prince, Seaman First Class, U.S. Navy, is missing following action in the performance of his duty and in the service of his country. The Department appreciates your great anxiety and will furnish you further information promptly when received. To prevent possible aid to our enemies, please do not divulge the name of his ship or station. Signed: Rear Admiral Randal Jacobs, Chief of the Bureau of Navigation. *(Information courtesy of the family of W. H. Prince)*

Seaman First Class Charles W. Prince of Spindale was listed as missing following the sinking of the U.S.S. *Houston*, which was lost in the Battle of Java; his parents, Mr. and Mrs. C. L. Prince were advised by the United States Navy Department.

Seaman First Class Prince was Rutherford County's sixth World War II casualty to date, including soldiers and sailors who have been killed in action or died of other causes. The county's casualties have been from the following localities: Harris, Caroleen, Cliffside, Rutherfordton, Chimney Rock and Spindale.

Seaman First Class Prince enlisted in the U.S. Navy at Spartanburg in July 1940. He was 21 years old and was born in Polk County. Prior to joining the U.S. Navy he was employed by Western Union Telegraph Company at Rutherfordton. (*Forest City Courier*, Big Issue, August 12, 1945)

The Presidential Unit Citation was presented to the U.S.S. *Houston*.

Information courtesy of the family of W. H. Prince and Helen Prince

Photos and information courtesy of <u>Daily Courier</u>, Forest City, North Carolina, James R. Brown, Publisher, W. H. Prince, and Helen Prince.

THE SECRETARY OF THE NAVY

WASHINGTON

The President of the United States takes pleasure in awarding the PRESIDENTIAL UNIT CITATION to the

UNITED STATES SHIP HOUSTON

for service as set forth in the following

CITATION:

"For outstanding performance against enemy Japanese forces in the Southwest Pacific from December 7, 1941 to February 28, 1942. At sea almost constantly, often damaged but self-maintaining, the HOUSTON kept the sea. She maneuvered superbly and with deadly anti-aircraft fire repulsed the nine-plane Japanese Bombing squadrons attacking a troop convoy under her escort. Later, in company with other Allied ships, she engaged a powerful enemy force, carried the brunt of the action with her two remaining 8 inch turrets and aided in damaging and routing two enemy heavy cruisers from the line of battle. On February 28, the HOUSTON went down, gallantly fighting to the last against overwhelming odds. She leaves behind her an inspiring record of valiant and distinguished service."

For the President,

Frank Knox
Secretary of the Navy.

RADFORD, LEROY
July 13, 1944

Mrs. Artence Radford of Spindale received a wire last week telling that her husband, Private First Class LeRoy Radford, 22, was killed in action in France, July 13, 1944. Private First Class Radford (1921-1944) of the U.S. Army was the son of Mr. and Mrs. Charles Radford of near Rutherfordton. (*Forest City Courier*, August 10, 1944)

RHODES, LAWRENCE M.
July 13, 1944

Private First Class Lawrence M. Rhodes, 22, was killed in action in France, July 13, according to a message to his parents, Mr. and Mrs. John Rhodes, Forest City, Route 1, Providence section. Private First Class Rhodes (February 8, 1922-July 13, 1944) of Henrietta and the U.S. Army went overseas in March of 1943 and entered the service December 21, 1942. His parents, a sister, and two brothers survived him. (*Rutherford County News*, August 17, 1944) He is buried in the Provident Methodist Church Cemetery. (http://rfci.net/wdfloyd/)

Photo courtesy of <u>*Daily Courier*</u>, *Forest City, North Carolina, and James R. Brown, Publisher*

RHODES, MARK ALEXANDER
December 7, 1941

Rutherford County's casualty list in World War II numbers 16 men. This includes all men who have died in service, were killed in action, or died accidentally.

Mark Alexander Rhodes, Seaman, U.S. Navy, of the Providence Community, Forest City, Route 1, was Rutherford County's first casualty. Seaman Rhodes (1920-1941) was killed in action when the ill-fated U.S.S. *Arizona* (BB-39) was sunk at Pearl Harbor in the treacherous attack on Sunday morning, December 7, 1941.

He was a son of Mr. and Mrs. Arthur Rhodes of Hendersonville and was the youngest of four brothers, all in the armed forces. He enlisted in the Navy in November of 1939 and was 21 years old at the time of his death.

He graduated from Harris High School in the class of 1938; after graduation he farmed for a short time and worked at the Alexander Manufacturing Company until his enlistment in the Navy.

The three brothers serving in the armed forces were David H. Rhodes, who had been in the U.S. Army 15 years; Chester A. Rhodes, in the U.S. Army four years; and Jay R. Rhodes, who for the past nine years had been in the U.S. Marine Corps. (*Forest City Courier*, August 12, 1945)

Photo courtesy of Daily Courier, Forest City, North Carolina, and James R. Brown, Publisher

Reading Left to Right: Mary Rhodes, Mark Rhodes, and Lorene Padgett Hopson

Photo courtesy of Lorene Padgett Hopson

ROBBINS, BRUCE CURTIS
January 3, 1945

Lieutenant Bruce C. Robbins, son of Mr. and Mrs. Lee R. Robbins of Bostic, was killed in action in Belgium on January 3, 1945, according to a message received by his parents Monday.

Lieutenant Robbins, an honor graduate of The Citadel, Charleston, South Carolina, class of 1943, volunteered for service in March of 1943 while he was still a student at The Citadel. He was commissioned at Fort Benning, Georgia, December 27, 1943, in the Infantry School, and later he entered the Paratroopers.

Lieutenant Robbins (April 9, 1923-January 3, 1945) went overseas August 17, 1944. He was 22 years old in April.

Surviving were his parents, his father being a prominent Bostic businessman and former chairman of the Rutherford County Board of Commissioners; and three sisters: Mrs. Lewis B. Johnson of Hamlet; Miss Lois Ann Robbins, a student at Converse College, Spartanburg, South Carolina; and Miriam Lee Robbins of Bostic.

Graduating with the highest honors of his class at The Citadel, he was very active in all phases of college activities. He was a member of the Citadel Band and symphony orchestra; served as a member of the editorial staff of *The Shako*, the college newspaper; and was a member and president of Gamma Alpha Mu. Lieutenant Robbins was a member of the Bostic Baptist Church. (*Forest City Courier*, January 25, 1945) He is buried in the Cool Springs Cemetery, Section #1. (http://rfci.net/wdfloyd/)

Materials courtesy of Lois Cole

ROBBINS, TURNER L.
December 6, 1944

Private Turner L. Robbins of the U.S. Army and of the Montford Cove section of Rutherford County was killed in action in France on December 6, according to a message received by his wife, Mrs. Estelle Robbins of Nebo.

Private Robbins, age 28, was survived by his wife; two small children, one son aged 6 and another son aged 18 months; his mother, Mrs. Margaret Robbins of Montford Cove, Union Mills, Route 1; two sisters: Mrs. John D. Wilkerson and Mrs. Lewis Parker of the Montford Cove community; two brothers: Green Robbins of Montford Cove and Technical Sergeant Five Walter Robbins, of Camp Lee, Virginia

Private Robbins (February 16, 1916-December 6,1944) had been overseas about 4 weeks. He trained at Camp Wheeler, Georgia. (*Forest City Courier*, December 28, 1944) He is buried in the Montford's Cove Baptist Cemetery. (http://rfci.net/wdfloyd/)

Photo courtesy of Pansy Parker

ROBERTSON, ROY A.
December 28, 1941

Funeral services for Second Lieutenant Roy A. Robertson, 27, who was fatally injured in the crash of a U.S. Army observation plane near Wrightsville Beach Saturday afternoon, were held at the home of his wife's parents near Union, South Carolina, Tuesday afternoon at 3 o'clock. He was the son of Mr. and Mrs. C. J. Robertson, of Caroleen.

Lieutenant Robertson (1914-1941) of the U.S. Army Air Forces was married to Miss Thesis Fowler on the morning of Christmas Eve.

He was making a routine patrol flight at the time of the crash, it was reported. Accompanying him was a gunner, Corporal Lewis Walker of Meridian, Mississippi, who was seriously injured.

Lieutenant Robertson was well known in this section. After finishing Tri-High School in Caroleen, he entered Wofford College, Spartanburg, where he graduated in 1936 after making a notable record in his studies and in athletics. The year following graduation he was named coach of the varsity basketball team and was identified with other Wofford College sports until he entered active service.

He finished his pilot training at Randolph Field, Texas, in August. He resigned an infantry commission to enter this branch of the service. (*Forest City Courier*, January 25, 1945)

Lieutenant Roy Robertson, Wofford graduate of 1936 and basketball coach of Wofford College until his resignation in 1941, was fatally injured December 27, when his observation plane crashed on the beach near Masonboro Inlet in the vicinity of Wrightsville Beach. Corporal Lewis Walker, gunner accompanying him, was seriously hurt.

Robertson, twenty-seven years old, died one hour and twenty minutes later as he was being ferried in a small boat to a waiting ambulance. His injuries were too serious to permit his being placed in another plane.

Robertson, whose parents lived in Caroleen, Rutherford County, North Carolina, was married on Christmas Eve to Miss Thesis Fowler of Union, South Carolina.

A star athlete at Wofford, Robertson made the All-State basketball team in his junior and senior years here. He received his flight training at Randolph Field, Texas and was called to service upon the completion of his training sometime last spring.

Robertson coached basketball teams recognized as being among the best in the State of South Carolina. During his short coaching career his teams were twice South Carolina's best in the S. I. A. A. conference, and in his last two years as coach they finished second in the State; they were behind Clemson and South Carolina in 1940 and 1941, respectively. (*Union Daily Times*, January 3, 1942)

A marker for Roy A. Robertson is in the Cool Springs Cemetery, Section # 2, Rutherford County, North Carolina. (http://rfci.net/wdfloyd/)

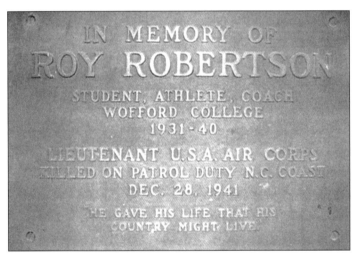

Marker at Wofford College in Memory of Roy Robertson

Photo of marker courtesy of Brigadier General Ed. Y. Hall

Entry for Roy Robertson from <u>Old Gold and Black</u>,
Wofford College, 1936

Roy Robertson, A. B.
Caroleen, N. C.
A.A.T. Blue Key. Scabbard and Blade
"It is not whether you win or lose, but how you play the game."

First Year: Football; Basketball; Baseball; Private R. O. T. C.;
   Preston Literary Society.

Second Year: President Sophomore Class; Varsity Football;
   Varsity Basketball; Varsity Track; Corporal R. O. T. C.;
   Honor Council; Preston Literary Society; Member N.C. Club;
   Executive Committee; Pan-Hellenie Council.

Third Year: Secretary of Student Body; Varsity Basketball;
   Varsity Baseball; Sergeant R.O.T.C.; Honor Council;
   Preston Literary Society; Secretary of North Carolina Club; Blue Key;
   Advisory Board Block "W" Club; Pan-Helline Council.

Fourth Year: President Student Body; Varsity Basketball;
   Varsity Baseball; Vice-President of Blue Key; President of
   North Carolina Club; Treasurer Block "W" Club; Honor Council;
   Preston Literary Society; Pan-Hellenie Council; Cadet Captain
   Assistant Personal Adjutant of R. O. T. C.; Member Scabbard
   and Blade; Member BOHEMIAN Staff; Carlisle Hall Advisory Board;
   Captain Basketball Team.

Article by Dr. H. N. Snyder as a Tribute to Roy Robertson
OLD GOLD AND BLACK
WOFFORD COLLEGE
JANUARY OF 1942

Roy . . .

By Dr. H. N. Snyder

We who teach are generally of the retiring, obscure people of the world. We do not make any great demands on life, knowing that its financial rewards are not for us, nor are those rewards that come from ambition for place and power. But we do have our satisfactions, and as we think of them we would not exchange them for those experiences that seem to give so much satisfaction to other people. Youth comes to us in its unripe, unformed days, remains with us a while, then leaves us, going out into life to meet its duties nobly and efficiently, accomplishing so much that is worthy as to bring to those who taught them feelings of pride and affection. We think that somehow we are a part of what they do.

Just ten years ago, a dark-haired, bright-eyed boy came to my office at Wofford College. Something about him—a frankness, an openness, a charm of personality—at once won me to him. Through four years we watched his unfolding growth into competent manhood as he enthusiastically shared in various Campus activities, at the same time meeting all his college duties in a highly satisfactory way.

Here was one we all knew we could love and trust, and we did. When he graduated in 1935 we brought him into our official family in an important position of leadership in the field of intercollegiate athletics, and for seven years, by his uprightness, his gentleness of speech and manner, his sturdy qualities of character, his willingness to help others, he placed himself deep in the heart of each of us, faculty and students.

And when his country needed him he promptly answered the call, dedicating his training, his youth, his hopes and his faith to preparing himself to protect for us the precious gifts and privileges of a free American in a menacing world. In defense of those dear things, he made the last sacrifice that men may make. Gallantly he gave his life that the rest of us and our children who come after us might live better and more safely under a flag that throws today over his young body its glorious folds as the symbol of his own gallantry.

Some day, somewhere, we shall the better understand the reasons for these experiences, because behind the shadow we must believe that the God of good causes and good men like Roy Robertson sitteth keeping watch above his own, and that the day will come when He will let us know that such sacrifice as this gallant young soldier of his country made, was not in vain. May the dear God of all grace and comfort be very close to all who loved him in these strange, dark hours, and may we, each of us, keep faith with the best as Roy did in the day of his youth!

RUPPE, LYNN T.
September 23, 1943

On Thursday afternoon, Mrs. Lula Ruppe of Cliffside received a telegram from the War Department notifying her that her son Private Lynn Ruppe was killed September 23, 1943, in Italy.

Private Ruppe entered the U.S. Army on July 27, 1942, at Fort McClellan, Alabama, and went to North Africa in December of 1942. He was a member of the infantry.

Private Ruppe would have been 20 years old on November 20. He (November 20, 1923-September 23, 1943) was survived by his mother; two sisters: Mrs. Alva Green and Miss Eloise Ruppe of Cliffside; four brothers: Donnis Ruppe in North Africa; Toy Ruppe in a U.S. Army camp in Louisiana; and Charlie and Roy Ruppe of Cliffside. (*Forest City Courier*, November 11, 1943)

RUPPE, TOY
September 13, 1944

Private First Class Toy Ruppe (1918-1944), U.S. Army, was killed in action in France on September 13, according to a message received by his mother, Mrs. Lula Ruppe of Cliffside. His brother Private Lynn Ruppe was killed in action in Italy on September 23, 1943, just short ten days of a year ago. This was the first instance of two war deaths in one family in Rutherford County during World War II.

Surviving were his mother; two sisters: Eloise Ruppe and Mrs. Alva Green of Cliffside; three brothers: Charles and Roy Ruppe of Cliffside; and Private Donnis E. Ruppe, U.S. Army in France. (*Forest City Courier*, December 28, 1944)

RUPPE, WILLIAM THOMAS
November 17, 1944

Private William Thomas Ruppe, 28, of the Shiloh Community, Rutherfordton, Route 1, died on November 17, 1944, of wounds received in military action on Leyte. The Reverend and Mrs. J. T. Ruppe, his grandparents, received the message from the War Department giving the news.

Private Ruppe, (February 10, 1920), a member of an Infantry Regiment of the U.S. Army, entered service on September 16, 1942, and had been overseas since April 22, 1943. He saw action in the Aleutians, Attu, and Marshall Islands.

His grandparents who reared him and one brother Burton Ruppe of Spindale survived Private Ruppe. Stonecutter Mill of Spindale employed Ruppe before he entered service. (*Forest City Courier*, October 5, 1944)

In a simple but impressive ceremony Sunday afternoon, the Silver Star awarded Private First Class William Thomas Ruppe (February 10, 1916-December 6, 1944) was presented posthumously to his grandparents, the Reverend and Mrs. J. T. Ruppe, at their home on West Street in North Spindale.

Colonel Wilbur J. Fox of Camp Croft, Spartanburg, South Carolina, presented the medal in the presence of the grandparents and a few friends; in a few brief and impressive words he explained the significance of the medal and the sacrifice made by Private First Class Ruppe. Reverend C. C. Matheny of Spencer Baptist Church conducted prayer.

Private First Class Ruppe was wounded in action in Leyte on November 15, 1944, and died November 17. He entered service in September of 1942 and had been overseas since April of 1943. He had seen action on Attu and in the Marshalls. He was awarded the Purple Heart in January of 1945.

Private First Class Ruppe was the son of Mr. and Mrs. John W. Ruppe and made his home with his grandparents in Livingston, Kentucky, until he entered the U.S. Army. His grandparents have been residents of Spindale for the past five months.

Following is an excerpt from a letter written by Captain David M. Hutchinson of the 17th Infantry, of which Private First Class Ruppe was a member, to the Reverend and Mrs. Ruppe:

On November 15, 1944, William's company was given a mission of driving the enemy from commanding ground on a ridge in the foothills west of Guinarona, Leyte Island. . .During this fierce fight which lasted for five hours in a downpour, William showed unusual courage and coolness under fire. With utter disregard for his personal safety, William advanced, thereby making the fire of the machine gun ineffective. Inspired by this example, his comrades rushed the enemy position and quickly eliminated it, thus contributing largely to the success of our mission. This action was hardly completed when William was wounded by sniper fire. . .However, his wounds were of too serious nature and he died. William was buried with full military honors in line with his religious faith in the Dulag Cemetery. . . .You will be glad to know that William has won the admiration of his officers and the respect and affection of his comrades by his sincerity, his courage, and his cheerfulness. (*Forest City Courier*, September 13, 1945)

Private First Class Ruppe is buried in the cemetery at Shiloh Baptist Church. (http://rfci.net/wdfloyd/)

Photos courtesy of
Jeanette Ruppe Taylor

SANE, MACK C.
April 4, 1945

Private Mark C. Sane (April 12, 1923-April 4, 1945) of the U.S. Army was killed in action in Germany on April 4, 1945. He had been overseas since January 1, 1944. He was a son of Mr. and Mrs. Fonzo B. Sane of near Rutherfordton. (*Forest City Courier*, May 3, 1945)

Funeral services for Private Sane were held at the Shiloh Baptist Church on Saturday, August 21, 1945, at 2:30 p.m. Pastor N. B. Phillips was in charge. He was assisted by the Reverend E. L. McDaniel and the Reverend R. L. Crawford. His cousins were flower girls and pallbearers.

The body of Private Sane arrived in Rutherfordton from a cemetery in St. Arnold, France. He entered the service in 1943 and received his military training at Fort Knox, Kentucky. He was almost 22 at the time of his death.

He was survived by his parents, Mr. and Mrs. F. B. Sane of the Shiloh Section; six sisters; and three brothers. (*Information courtesy of Jeanette Ruppe Taylor*)

His family consisted of John B. Sane (1914), Annie Bess Sane Henson (1916), Louis W. Sane (1918), Pearl Rae Sane Wall (1921), Mack C. Sane (1923), Blanche Sane (1925), Margaret Sane (1928), Bill Sane (1930), and the twins Jacqueline (Jack) Sane and Josephine (Jo) Sane, born in 1932. (*Information courtesy of Pearl Wall*)

Mack Joined Grey's Creek Baptist Church at the age of 20. He served in Company B, 47th Tank Battalion. He enjoyed a wide circle of friends and relatives and gave his life for his country. Mack had two brothers (Louis W. and John B.) who served overseas. *(Information courtesy of Jeanette Ruppe Taylor)*

Private Sane was the Top Gunner in a tank attempting to cross the Rhine River. When a hand grenade entered the tank, both Sane and his commander were killed. *(Information courtesy of Pearl Wall)*

Photos courtesy of <u>Daily Courier</u>, Forest City, North Carolina; James R. Brown, Publisher; and Jeanette Ruppe Taylor

SCHWARTZ, CARL JACOB
March 1945

Private First Class Carl Jacob Schwartz, aged 20, son of Mr. and Mrs. F. L. Schwartz of Avondale, died of wounds received in action on Iwo Jima, according to a message received Sunday by his parents.

Young Schwartz entered the U.S. Marines Corps June 7, 1943, and had been overseas since November 27, 1944.

He was survived by his parents; one brother, Laird Schwartz, Jr.; and six sisters: Virginia, Peggy, Catherine, Martha, Geraldine, and Hattie Mae, all at home. He was the oldest of the eight children. (*Forest City Courier*, April 12, 1945)

Photo courtesy of <u>Daily Courier</u>, Forest City, North Carolina, and James R. Brown, Publisher

SCRUGGS, BOYCE P., JR.
April 10, 1945

Dr. and Mrs. B. P. Scruggs of Rutherfordton received word that their son Flight Officer Boyce P. Scruggs, Jr., who was reported missing during a flight over Germany on April 10, 1945, was presumed to be dead.

Flight Officer Scruggs was Co-Pilot on a B-17 airplane that participated in a bombing mission over Oranienburg, Germany, on the date he was reported missing. His plane collided in midair with another plane of the same formation, while coming off the bomb run, approximately sixty miles north of Berlin. One crew member of the other plane parachuted to safety and reported that Lieutenant Scruggs' plane exploded in midair and that none of the crew survived.

Flight Officer Scruggs (1925-1945) was the only son of Dr. and Mrs. B. P. Scruggs. He graduated from Central High School in the class of 1942 and entered the University of North Carolina in the fall of that year; he remained at the University of North Carolina until he entered the Military Service as Aviation Cadet at Keesler Field, Mississippi, during the summer of 1943.

From Keesler Field he went to Texas Tech College, Lubbock, Texas, and to Santa Ana, California, where he received his preflight training. His primary training was received at Wickenburg, Arizona, basic flying at Bakersfield, California; he took his advanced flying training at Douglas Army Air Field, Douglas, Arizona. It was there that he received his Pilot's Wings and was appointed Flight Officer in the Army Air Corps in August of 1944. His final training in air combat was taken at Drew Field.

Flight Officer Scruggs (1925-1945) went overseas during the latter part of February of 1945. He was a member of the 305th Bombardment

Group of the Eighth Air Force and was serving as co-pilot on a B-17 Bomber on his seventh mission over enemy territory when his plane was shot down with the loss of the entire crew.

Surviving Flight Officer Scruggs are his parents and two sisters: Miss Catherine Scruggs, a student at Limestone College, and Miss Ann Scruggs at home. He was a nephew of Dr. Marvin Scruggs, Dr. W. N. Scruggs, Dr. C. J. Scruggs, and Captain R. R. Scruggs of Cleveland, Ohio. (*Forest City Courier*, April 18, 1946)

Photo courtesy of Daily Courier, Forest City, North Carolina, and James R. Brown, Publisher

SHELTON, EVERETT A.
October 12, 1944

Staff Sergeant Everett A. Shelton of Rutherfordton, Route 3, was killed in action in Germany on October 12, according to a message received by his mother, Mrs. E. M. Shelton.

Sergeant Shelton (March 1, 1925-October 12, 1944) entered the U.S. Army on March 3, 1941, at Fort Benning, Georgia, and was sent to North Africa December 25, 1942. He participated in the invasion of North Africa, Sicily, and France and spent two weeks in Belgium and three days in Holland; his outfit was the first to land on Belgian soil.

One brother, who was in the U.S. Army and stationed in France; his parents, Mr. and Mrs. E. M. Shelton of Rutherfordton, Route 3; and a sister survived him. (*Forest City Courier*, November 9, 1944) He is buried in the Rutherfordton City Cemetery, Section #4. (http://rfci.net/wdfloyd/)

SHELTON, JAMES W.
October 4, 1944

Private James W. Shelton was missing in action in France since October 4, according to telegram received by his wife, Mrs. Ellen Christine Shelton. He was with the infantry in France. He entered service in March of 1943, trained at Camp Wallace, Texas, and Camp Maxey, Texas. He went overseas in August of 1944.

Private Shelton (August 17, 1924-October 4, 1944) was the son of Mrs. Louise Connor of Rutherford County and Lester Shelton of Whitmire, South Carolina. In 1942 he was married to Ellen Roberts of Griffin, Georgia, and they have a daughter, Joanne, aged two years. (*Forest City Courier*, November 9, 1944)

Note: The War Department declared later that Private James W. Shelton was killed on October 4, 1944. He is buried in the Rutherfordton City Cemetery, Section #4. (http://rfci.net/wdfloyd/)

SIGMON, CLAUDIUS
May 2, 1945

Sergeant Claudius Sigmon, son of Mr. Peter L. Sigmon of Ellenboro, North Carolina, has been promoted to Staff Sergeant. A member of Company C, 152nd Infantry, he saw action in the 38th Division's 16-day battle for strategic and heavily fortified Zig Zag Pass, east of Olongapo. This action opened another route to Manila. Overseas for 16 months, he served previously in Hawaii, New Guinea, and Leyte. *(Courtesy of Sue Toms; Daily Courier, Forest City, North Carolina; and James R. Brown, Publisher)*

Staff Sergeant Claudius Sigmon (1913-1945) of Ellenboro was killed in action on Luzon in the Phillippines on May 2, 1945, according to a message received by his parents, Mr. and Mrs. P. L. Sigmon of Ellenboro.

A member of an Infantry Regiment, he entered service on October 6, 1942, and had been overseas since January 1944. He was wounded in action on February 12, for which he received the Purple Heart. On April 18, he was awarded the Bronze Star.

He is survived by his parents and eight sisters. *(Courtesy of Sue Toms)*

Photo courtesy of <u>Daily Courier</u>, Forest City, North Carolina, and James R. Brown, Publisher

SIMPSON, JOHN A., JR.
1945

Rutherford County's casualty list for the week shows four more casualties, two dead and two wounded. This brought Rutherford County's total casualty list for World War II to 109 dead, 38 prisoners of war, and 20 missing.

Mr. and Mrs. John A. Simpson of Rutherfordton have received a message from the War Department. The message notified them that their son Sergeant John A. Simpson, Jr., aged 19, was killed in action on Iwo Jima Island. He entered service May 2, 1942, and had been overseas for some time. A special memorial service was held in the Rutherfordton Presbyterian Church Sunday at 5 o'clock. (*Rutherford County News*, April 19, 1945)

SISK, CRAIG
July 16, 1944

Staff Sergeant Craig Sisk, 29, was killed in action in France, July 16, according to a message received Monday by his wife, Mrs. Fannie Sisk of Brevard. He was a son of Mrs. Bessie Sisk of Bostic and was a member of the first group of trainees to leave Rutherford County in 1941. He had been overseas five months with the U.S. Army.

Staff Sergeant Craig Sisk (1915-1944) was survived by his mother; his wife; four brothers: Max Sisk, U.S. Army, Camp Gruber, Okla.; Carl Sisk, U.S. Army, stationed in England; Woodrow Sisk, Forest City, and P. R. Sisk, Burnsville; four sisters: Mrs. Bell Harris, Bostic; Mrs. Annie Harris, Forest City; Mrs. May Patton, Robbinsville; and Miss Nettie Sisk of Shelby. (*Rutherford County News*, August 10, 1944)

Sergeant Sisk, son of Mrs. Bessie Sisk of Bostic, entered the U.S. Army on January 22, 1941. (*Forest City Courier*, Big Issue, August 12, 1945)

Photo courtesy of Max Sisk

Photo courtesy of <u>Daily Courier</u>, Forest City, North Carolina, and James R. Brown, Publisher

SISK, DAZEL WILLIAMS, SR.
February 8. 1945

Private First Class Dazel Williams Sisk, Sr., (October 30, 1922-February 8, 1945) of the U.S. Army and originally from Rutherfordton, was killed in Germany on February 8, 1945. *(Nancy Stallcup's Memorial Honor Roll)* His body is interred in the Rutherfordton City Cemetery. (http://rfci.net/wdfloyd/)

Private First Class Sisk of Rutherfordton had been missing in action in Germany since February 8, 1945, according to a message received by his wife, Mrs. Doris Lovelace Sisk of Rutherfordton. He had entered service in June of 1945 and went overseas in November of 1944. (*Forest City Courier*, March 22, 1945)

Private First Class Dazel Williams Sisk, Sr., of Rutherfordton, reported missing in action in Germany in February of 1945, is dead, according to a message received on Sunday by his wife, Mrs. Doris Lovelace Sisk of Rutherfordton.

The death of Private First Class Sisk brings Rutherford County's total casualty list of World War II to 114 dead.

Private First Class Sisk had been in service two years and went overseas with an Infantry Regiment on December 13, 1944. He was reported missing in action in Germany on February 8, 1945. The telegram confirmed his death as of that date.

Private First Class Sisk is survived by his wife; a two-year-old son; his parents: Mr. and Mrs. D. M. Sisk of Rutherfordton; and several brothers and sisters. (*Forest City Courier*, June 14, 1945)

SMITH, JAMES L.
April 22, 1945

Staff Sergeant James L. Smith, son of Mr. and Mrs. Ernest L. Smith of Spindale, was killed in action on April 22, 1945, in Germany. He was reported missing in action on that date, and the second message yesterday confirmed his death.

A member of an Infantry Regiment of the U.S. Army, Staff Sergeant Smith (1922-1945) entered service in April of 1943 and went overseas in September of 1944. He graduated from Fairforest High School, near Spartanburg, South Carolina, and for some time Spindale Mill employed him; after his employment, he entered North Carolina State College at Raleigh.

His parents; two brothers: Harold Smith, Greenville, South Carolina; First Lieutenant W. E. Smith, Orlando, Florida, and one sister, Miss Ernestine, a student at the Woman's College, University of North Carolina at Greensboro, survived him. (*Forest City Courier*, May 24, 1945)

SMITH, LEONARD
November 6, 1944

Private First Class Leonard Smith, aged 26, of Harris, was killed in a vehicle accident at Camp Chaffee, Arkansas, Monday, according to a message received today by his mother, Mrs. Nancy Smith of Harris.

No details of the accident were received. Private Smith's body (April 8, 1916-November 6, 1944) was shipped to Harris for funeral services. He entered the U.S. Army on June 10, 1941, and was attached to the field artillery. He was a son of Mrs. Smith and the late William Smith of Harris. He was survived by his mother; four brothers: Roy, Ted and Houston Smith of Harris, and Private Martin Smith of Fort Benning, Georgia; and one sister, Mrs. Alice Tipton of the Shiloh Community, Rutherfordton, Route 1.

Funeral arrangements will be made pending the arrival of the body from Arkansas. (*Forest City Courier*, November 9, 1944) He is buried in the Broad River Baptist Church Cemetery. (http://rfci.net/wdfloyd/)

SMITH, RALPH C.
April 12, 1943

Mrs. Mary Helen Smith of Spindale received a message on April 13, 1943, from the War Department. The announcement stated that her husband Private Ralph C. Smith (1921-1943) of the U.S. Army Air Forces died April 12, 1943, in the Western Pacific combat zone. Later she was informed that he met death by the accidental explosion of a bomb. He was 21 years old and was a son of Mr. and Mrs. Cecil Smith of Spindale. (*Forest City Courier*, Big Issue, August 12, 1945, *Forest City Courier*, December 16, 1943)

Photo courtesy of <u>*Daily Courier,*</u> *Forest City, North Carolina, and James R. Brown, Publisher*

STULL, EUGENE S., III

Second Lieutenant Eugene S. Stull, III, of the U.S. Army and of Rutherford County gave his life during World War II. *(Nancy Stallcup's Memorial Honor Roll)*

SUTTLE, FLOYD L.
September 23, 1944

Private First Class Floyd L. Suttle, aged 34, was killed in Holland on September 23, according to a message received by his brother Percy Suttle of Union Mills community.

Private First Class Suttle of the U.S. Army was survived by three brothers: Percy; R. E. Suttle of Brevard; Columbus Suttle, Cooper's Gap; and two sisters: Mrs. Sadie McCurry, Rutherfordton; and Mrs. Addie Littlejohn, Green Hill. (*Forest City Courier*, November 9, 1944)

SWINK, EDGAR T.
June 26, 1944

Private Edgar T. Swink, aged 27, of Ellenboro, Route 1, was killed in action in France on June 26, 1944, according to a message received by his parents, Mr. and Mrs. P. L. Swink, also of Ellenboro, Route 1. Private Swink entered the U.S. Army in June of 1942; he had been overseas five months with an Infantry Division.

Private Swink (December 11, 1917-June 26, 1944) was survived by his parents; three brothers: Private Grady Swink, stationed in New Guinea; Jean and Cecil Swink at home; and one sister: Mrs. Melson

Dixon of Avondale. (*The Rutherford County News*, August 10, 1944) He is buried in the Sandy Plains Baptist Cemetery, Cleveland County. (http://rfci.net/wdfloyd/)

*Photos courtesy of
Mr. and Mrs. Grady Swink*

TATE, BAXTER WISEMAN
June 16, 1944

Mrs. F. B. Tate of Henrietta received word from the War Department that her son Staff Sergeant Baxter Wiseman Tate, aged 42, died in Algeria, North Africa on June 16.

Staff Sergeant Tate (January 21, 1902-June 16, 1944) had served in the U.S. Army for 23 years and had been overseas about three and one-half months at the time of his death.

Surviving beside his mother were his widow and young son, who reside in Paris, Texas; four brothers, one of whom was serving with the Marines in the South Pacific; and seven sisters. (*Rutherford County News*, August 10, 1944/*Forest City Courier*, August 24, 1944) He is buried in the Floyds Creek Baptist Cemetery. (http://rfci.net/wdfloyd/)

Photo courtesy of Daily Courier, Forest City, North Carolina, and James R. Brown, Publisher

TAYLOR, JAMES B.

Private First Class James B. Taylor of the U.S. Army and of Rutherford County gave his life during World War II. *(Nancy Stallcup's Memorial Honor Roll)*

TESSNEAR, RICHARD C.
July 14, 1944

Private Richard C. Tessnear, son of B. R. Tessnear of Ellenboro, Route 2, died of wounds received in the Battle of the Marshall Islands, according to a wire from the War Department to his parents last week. (*Rutherford County News*, August 3, 1944)

Mr. and Mrs. B. R. Tessnear of Mooresboro, Route 1, had five sons in the armed service of the United States. Private Richard C. Tessnear was recently killed in action.

Private Emmett Tessnear, aged 29, entered service March 13, 1944, and took his basic training at Camp Wheeler, Georgia, where he was stationed. Private Ernest Tessnear, 27, entered service in August, 1942, was trained at Fort Jackson, South Carolina, and was stationed at Fort Riley, Kansas. Private Timer Tessnear, 24, entered service December 5, 1942. He trained at Fort Bragg. He was at Camp Shelby, Mississippi. Richard C. Tessnear, 22, entered service December 27, 1942, trained at Camp Croft, South Carolina, as a member of an Infantry Brigade. He was killed in action in France last month. Harry S. Tessnear, 19, entered service May 13, 1944, and took his training at Fort Sill, Oklahoma. (*Forest City Courier*, August 17, 1944)

Photo courtesy of Timer Tessnear

Five Brothers Served in World War II

Private Emmett Tessnear   *Private Ernest Tessnear*   *Private Timer Tessnear*

Private Richard Tessnear   *Private Harry S. Tessnear*

Photos Courtesy of <u>*Daily Courier*</u>*, Forest City, North Carolina, and James R. Brown, Publisher*

THORNE, BENJAMIN TILLMAN
May 1943

The results of this worldwide war were brought closer to Rutherford County Friday when a wire from Washington, D.C., stated that Private First Class Ben Tillman Thorne "died as a result of injuries received in action." The wire came to his mother, Mrs. Addie Thorne; the message stated a letter would follow which to date had not arrived.

Private First Class Thorne (1925-1943) was the youngest son of the Reverend and Mrs. J. L. Thorne. He volunteered in January of 1942 at the age of 16 and joined the U.S. Marine Corps. He was in the Fifth Marines. He had seen action in the South Pacific and was on Guadalcanal from May of 1942 to January of 1943. His mother received a letter from him on May 24; written May 14, the letter stated that he was O.K.

Private First Class Ben Tillman Thorne was wounded between May 14 and May 28. He was somewhere in the South Pacific. He was the youngest man in the Fifth Marines. He last visited his mother on Mother's Day in May of 1942. He had a brother, Albert Henry Thorne, who was in the Navy and stationed at Pensacola, Florida. (*The Rutherford County News*, June 3, 1943/*Forest City Courier*, Big Issue, August 12, 1943)

Photos courtesy of Daily Courier, Forest City, North Carolina, and James R. Brown, Publisher

TINSLEY, FRED P.
January 17, 1945

Sergeant Fred P. Tinsley, son of Mr. and Mrs. J. J. Tinsley of Forest City, was reported missing in action in France since January 17, 1945. He was attached to a Tank Battalion of the U.S. Army.

Sergeant Tinsley (1915-1945) received his training at Camp Chaffee, Arkansas, and Camp Campbell, Kentucky. He went overseas in October 1944 and landed in southern France. He entered service in December of 1942.

A twin brother, Private Thomas Frank Tinsely, was recently inducted into the U.S. Army. Thomas Frank Tinsley took his basic training at Camp Blanding, Florida. His wife and daughters made their home in Hickory, North Carolina. (*Forest City Courier*, February 22, 1945)

Sergeant Fred Tinsley, aged 30, who was reported missing in action in Germany on January 17, 1945, died in action on that date, according to a message received from the War Department by his parents, Mr. and Mrs. J. J. Tinsley of Forest City.

Sergeant Tinsley's death brought Rutherford County's total World War II dead to 123 men, with five carried on military rolls as missing in action.

Sergeant Tinsley, a member of the Tank Corps, entered service in October of 1942, was trained at Camp Chaffee, Arkansas, and Camp Campbell, Tennessee, and went overseas in September of 1944. He was a graduate of Cool Springs High School of Forest City.

His parents; six brothers: Herbert L. Tinsley, Washington, D.C.; John M. and Al. S. Tinsley, Covington, Louisiana; Joe W. Tinsley, Camp Lejuene, North Carolina; Private Frank Tinsley, a twin brother, at Fort Meade, Maryland; Staff Sergeant Jack Tinsley, in France; and two sisters: Mrs. Troy Geer of Forest City and Mrs. D. A. Blue, Southern Pines, survived Sergeant Tinsley. (*Forest City Courier*, February 22, 1945)

Photo courtesy of <u>Daily Courier</u>, Forest City, North Carolina, and James R. Brown, Publisher

TOLLESON, JAMES BRUCE
July 17, 1945

Staff Sergeant James Bruce Tolleson, son of Mr. and Mrs. Max Tolleson, of Rutherfordton, Star Route, was believed to have died in the crash of his plane, a B-29 bomber, on Halmahera Island on the morning of July 17, according to letters received by his parents from his commanding officer and from the Chaplain of his squadron. He was previously reported missing in action by the War Department.

A letter from Captain Townsend Rogers, his immediate commanding officer, said:

> The plane of which your son was a gunner, took off from the Pitoe Air Strip, Morotai Island at 3:39 o'clock on the morning of 17 July of 1945, on a strike mission against the enemy. The aircraft was seen to make a normal take-off and depart on that course. No radio contact could be made with the plane after take-off and extensive searches were conducted after it was determined that the aircraft was not returning from the mission. One survivor of the crew made his way to Allied territory after a period of several days. He reported that the aircraft crashed into a mountain on Halmahera Island and exploded and burst into flames. He was thrown clear of the plane, but because of his dazed condition at the time, he could not tell if any of the others were safe. The crash took place in enemy-held territory, and as he knew the explosion would bring any Japanese in the near vicinity, he could not remain and try to locate any other survivors.

A letter from Captain Garland E. Hopkins, chaplain, says:

> The plane on which Sergeant Tolleson was a member of the crew crashed into a mountain in the Halmaheras a few minutes after the take-off. The plane burned immediately and the ammu-

nition and bombs it was carrying exploded. The sole survivor of the crash was Staff Sergeant Richard H. Rutledge, who like Sergeant Tolleson was not a member of this crew but was flying with them that day. I personally talked with Staff Sergeant Rutledge and asked him what he thought of the possibility of the survival of the other members of the crew. He said he was so stunned and dazed that he could not know for sure what happened after the crash. However, he doubted very strongly that any of the others could have survived. I wish I might be able to give you more hopeful news, and indeed there is always a measure of hope which one may keep alive. However, I think it would be wrong for me to give you any undue encouragement since the natives who found and brought back Sergeant Rutledge were friendly and would probably have immediately brought in any other survivors.

Brigadier General Leon W. Johnson has written:

Sergeant Tolleson was a gunner on a B-24 Liberator bomber which participated in a combat mission to Borneo on Morotai Island. Sergeant Tolleson's bomber encountered adverse weather and crashed in a mountainous region located on the northern tip of Halmahera Island in the Netherlands Indies. Also as soon as it was apparent the plane was missing, a thorough and extensive search was made for this aircraft, but all results were negative.

Sergeant Tolleson (December 7, 1925-July 17, 1945) was the only son of Mr. and Mrs. Max Tolleson. He was a grandson of Mrs. L. W. Griffin of Spindale. He entered the U.S. Army Air Forces on January 6, 1944, while a student at Clemson College, South Carolina. He had been with the Thirteenth Army Air Forces in the South Pacific since January of 1945; he had expected to return home soon. He was awarded the Air Medal for "meritorious achievement while participating in aerial flight in the Southwest Pacific area from February 17, 1945 to April 9, 1945." He also held several other medals; his unit held six Battle Stars. He was 20 years old. (*Forest City Courier*, June 28, 1945)

Sergeant Bruce Tolleson, son of Mr. and Mrs. Max Tolleson of Rutherfordton, Star Route, was missing in action, according to a message received by his parents.

195

Sergeant Tolleson was missing since July 17 over Borneo according to the message. He had been in that theatre of action with the Thirteenth Army Air Forces since January of 1945. He had written that he expected to be sent home soon.

Sergeant Tolleson, 20 years old, entered service January 6, 1944, while he was a student at Clemson College.

Sergeant Tolleson was recently awarded the Air Medal for "meritorious achievement while participating in aerial flight in the Southwest Pacific area from February 17, 1945, to April of 1945. These flights included bombing missions against enemy installations, shipping and supply bases and aided considerably in the recent successes in that theatre."

He also held several medals and was a member of a unit awarded six Battle Stars. (*Forest City Courier*, August 2, 1945)

Staff Sergeant James Bruce Tolleson, 20, son of Mr. and Mrs. Max Tolleson of Rutherfordton, Star Route, died in action on July 17, 1945, according to a message received today by his parents.

A member of the Thirteenth Air Force's Famous "Snooper" Squad, a daredevil group of aerialists who terrorized the enemy by their "hedge-hopping" fighting, Sergeant Tolleson died when his plane crashed into a mountain on Halmahera Island, one of the Borneo group of islands.

The parents had previously been notified that he was missing in action. The telegram from the War Department stated:

> The Secretary of War has asked me to express his deep regret that your son Staff Sergeant James Bruce Tolleson was killed in action over Borneo July 17, 1945. He was previously reported missing in action. I regret that unavoidable circumstances made necessary the unusual lapse of time in reporting your son's death to you.

Sergeant Tolleson's death brings Rutherford County's World War II toll to 131 dead and two still carried on the U. S. Army's roster as missing in action.

Sergeant Tolleson was born December 7, 1925, at Spindale. He graduated from Ford High School, Laurens, South Carolina, with the Class of 1942 and entered Clemson College in September of 1942. He entered the service January 6, 1944, while a student at Clemson, and went into the Borneo Theatre of Action in January of 1945. At the time of his death, he was flying an extra mission, having already made more than forty missions over enemy-occupied territory; he expected to return home soon.

He was awarded the Air Medal for "meritorious achievement while participating in aerial flight in the Southwest Pacific area from February 17, 1945, to April 9, 1945.

These flights included bombing missions against enemy installations, shipping and supply bases and aided considerably in recent successes in that theatre." He also held several medals; his unit held six Battle Stars.

Sergeant Tolleson is survived by his parents and his grandmother, Mrs. Lewis W. Griffin, of Spindale. (*Forest City Courier*, March 7, 1946)

Photos Courtesy of Daily Courier, Forest City, North Carolina, and James R. Brown, Publisher

WARD, ROBERT "BOB"
August 10, 1944

Private First Class Robert "Bob" Ward (1924-1944), son of Mrs. H. C. Ward and the late Mr. Ward of Caroleen, was killed in action in France on August 10, 1944, according to a message received from the War Department Friday. Private First Class Ward (March 20, 1924-August 10, 1944) entered the U.S. Army on January 27, 1943, and went overseas in May of 1943. He remained in England until June 6.

Private First Class Ward, age 20, was survived by his mother; four brothers: Roy Ward, Gastonia; Private First Class Leon Ward of Fort Monmouth; J. J., Charles, and Daytus Ward of Caroleen; and three sisters: Mrs. Q. Teseniar and Misses Peggy and Patsy Ward of Caroleen. (*Forest City Courie*r, August 31, 1944)

Private First Class Ward's body is interred in the Avondale Cemetery. (http://rfci.net/wdfloyd/)

Photo courtesy of <u>Daily Courier</u>, Forest City, North Carolina, and James R. Brown, Publisher

WAYCASTER, RALPH WALDEN
April 16, 1945

Private First Class Ralph Walden Waycaster was killed in action in Germany on April 16, 1945, according to a telegram from the War Department. His parents, Mr. and Mrs. G. W. Waycaster of Avondale, received the telegram on Saturday.

Private First Class Waycaster (August 18, 1919-April 16, 1945) was inducted into the U. S. Army on December 5, 1942, and received his training at Camp Chaffee, Arkansas, and Camp Campbell, Kentucky; he spent several months on maneuvers in Tennessee.

He went overseas in September of 1944 as an M. P. with the 14th Armored Division, attached to the Seventh Army, and had been in combat service in France and Germany.

His parents; two sisters: Mrs. Ed Wagoner of Tryon and Miss Grace Waycaster of Avondale; and three brothers: Frank Waycaster of Marion; Lawrence and Claude Waycaster of Avondale survived him. (*Forest City Courier*, May 3, 1945)

The Bronze Star Medal was awarded posthumously to Private First Class Ralph Waycaster, son of Mr. and Mrs. G. W. Waycaster of Avondale. Private First Class Waycaster was killed in action April 16, 1945, while serving with the military police in Germany.

The award made by direction of the President will be presented to Private First Class Waycaster's parents at a time and date to be determined later. The citation reads:

> For meritorious service in France and Germany from October 21, 1944, to April 16, 1945. The initiative, efficiency and alertness, which Private First Class Waycaster repeatedly demonstrated throughout this period, enabled him to carry out each of the varied duties to which he was assigned in an exemplary manner. His unusual versatility as well as his tireless devotion to duty were inspirational to those associated with him and reflect credit on him and the armed forces. (*Forest City Courier*, October 25, 1945)

Memorial services were held at Temple Baptist Church Sunday afternoon at 3:30 o'clock for Private First Class Ralph W. Waycaster, who was killed in action in Germany on April 16.

The Reverend F. E. Dabney, pastor, was in charge of the service and was assisted by the Reverend S. L. Lamm of Avondale and Chaplain J. E. Scott of Charlotte. Mr. Charlie Greene directed the choir, with Miss Ellen Padgette as pianist. "Amazing Grace," and "Have Faith in God" were the songs sung. Mrs. F. E. Dabney sang "Beautiful Isle of Somewhere" as a solo.

The Reverend Dabney read appropriate scripture passages and led in the prayers. The Reverend Lamm spoke words of comfort to the family. Chaplain Scott, in a very sympathetic manner, spoke comforting words to the members of the family and relatives; he eulogized the deceased as a hero, who had died for a good cause.

Private First Class Waycaster was born August 18, 1919. He attended the public schools of Spruce Pine and Henrietta. He was an amiable person of admirable qualities and had scores of friends who were deeply touched by his untimely death and the supreme sacrifice he made by giving his life for his country.

While a resident of Henrietta, he was a faithful attendant of High Shoals Baptist Church and was a member of the Young Men's Bible class of the Sunday School. In 1938, he made a profession of faith, during the pastorate of the Reverend H. L. Phillips.

Ralph entered the U.S. Army at Fort Bragg, December 5, 1942, and received his basic training at Camp Chaffee, Arkansas, with the Fourteenth Armored Division as a tank driver.

Later he was transferred to the Military Police. After completing training in this branch of service, he was sent on maneuvers in Tennessee on November 12, 1943. During this period he was commended for his efficiency as a Military Police Officer in Clarksville, Tennessee, and Hopkinsville, Kentucky. On January 24, 1944, his company was moved to Camp Campbell, Kentucky.

Protestant Chaplain Hollingsworth officiated at the military funeral service held for Private First Class Waycaster. The earthly remains of Ralph W. Waycaster lie buried in the United States Military Cemetery at Bensheim, Germany.

His survivors were: his parents, Mr. and Mrs. G. W. Waycaster of Avondale; two sisters: Mrs. Ed Wagoner of Tryon and Miss Grace Waycaster of Avondale; three brothers: Frank of Marion, Lawrence and Claude Waycaster of Avondale; and a number of nieces and nephews. (*Forest City Courier*, May 3, 1945)

His body is interred in the Avondale Cemetery. (http://rfci.net/wdfloyd/)

WELLS, THOMAS WOODROW
February 16, 1944

The war got even closer to Rutherford County in February of 1944. Technical Sergeant Five Thomas Woodrow Wells was killed in action on February 16, 1944, in Italy.

Sunday a wire from the Adjutant General's office in Washington, D. C., came to his parents, Mr. and Mrs. Rolan T. Wells, Cane Creek section, Morganton highway, Union Mills, Route 2. The message stated: "Technical Five Sergeant Thomas W. Wells was killed in action in defense of his country on February 16 in Italy."

Technical Sergeant Five Wells, 27, had been overseas about a year. He had been in the U.S. Army two years. He was in the North African campaign. His family received a letter from him February 14. He wrote the letter on January 13 and stated he was O.K. (*Rutherford County News*, March 16, 1944)

Technical Sergeant Five Thomas W. Wells (January 28, 1917-February 16, 1944) was killed in Italy in action on February 16, 1944. He was driving a tank and was killed instantly. He was the son of Mr. and Mrs. Rolan T. Wells, Cane Creek section, Morganton highway, Union Mills, Route 2. He was in the North African campaign. (*Rutherford County News*, May 25, 1944)

Technical Sergeant Five Thomas W. Wells's body is interred in the Sandy Level Baptist Church Cemetery. (http://rfci.net/wdfloyd/)

Photos courtesy of <u>*Daily Courier*</u>*, Forest City, North Carolina, and James R. Brown, Publisher*

WHITESIDE, RANSOME J.
March 4, 1943

Private Ransome Whiteside of the U.S. Army, originally from Uree, died suddenly on March 4, 1943, at Camp Gordon, near Augusta, Georgia. He was a son of Mr. and Mrs. Harold Whiteside of the Uree community near Chimney Rock. His body was returned to Rutherford County and interred in Bill's Creek Cemetery with full military honors. (*Forest City Courier*, Big Issue, August 12, 1943/*Forest City Courier*, December 16, 1943)

Private Whiteside (1921-1943) was given a full military funeral at camp; his father and two brothers-in-law attended the services. The body was brought to Rutherfordton and burial services conducted at Bill's Creek Baptist Church Wednesday morning where many friends joined the family in paying a last tribute to this young man who gave his life for his country. (*Rutherford County News*, March 11, 1943)

WILLIAMS, HERMAN JOHN
November 12, 1944

Sergeant Herman John Williams, 25, eldest son of Mr. and Mrs. John H. Williams of the Green Hill Community, west of Rutherfordton, was killed in action in the Pacific on November 12, according to a message from the War Department.

Sergeant Wells (1919-1944) of the U.S. Army had been overseas nearly three years and had served in New Guinea, Australia, and other points in the South and Southwest Pacific. He was killed in action on Leyte Island.

He was survived by his parents, Mr. and Mrs. Williams; two brothers: Fred of the U.S. Army and stationed at Maxton, North Carolina, and Byron Williams at home; and one sister, Miss Ola Williams, nurses' training corps, Rutherfordton. He was a grandson of the late Sheriff W. C. Hardin. (*Forest City Courier*, December 21, 1944)

WILSON, DARRELL JUSTICE
June 9, 1944

Darrell Justice Wilson, Boatswain's Mate Second Class, 19, son of A. D. Wilson, Avondale, was missing in action. He had been overseas 9 months and in service nearly 20 months. (*Rutherford County News*, August 10, 1944)

Mr. and Mrs. A. D. Wilson of Avondale received a message Friday from the Navy Department informing them that their son Darrell Justice Wilson, Boatswain's Mate Second Class, was killed in action in France on June 9, 1944.

Boatswain's Mate Second Class Wilson (1925-1944) was previously reported as missing following action in the performance of his duty and in the service of his country. He was 19 years of age. He enrolled in the U.S. Naval Reserves on January 21, 1943, and took his basic training at Bainbridge, Maryland, and at Little Creek, Virginia. He had been overseas about nine months. He was reported missing in action last month.

Photo courtesy of <u>Daily Courier</u>, Forest City, North Carolina, and James R. Brown, Publisher

He was survived by his parents and three sisters, Miss Lois Wilson, Avondale; Mrs. Albert Allen of Charlotte; and Mrs. Robert E. Davis of Norfolk, Virginia. He was a graduate of Tri-High School.

Memorial services for him will be held next Sunday afternoon at Haynes Memorial Baptist Church, Avondale, with his pastor officiating. He was a member of that church. (*Forest City Courier*, August 31, 1944)

Mrs. Margaret Allen reported in December of 2002 that she had received word of her brother's death (Darrell Justice Wilson, Boatswain's Mate Second Class) and that her husband, Albert Allen, received word of the death of his brother Private Jack Allen in the same week.

*Photo and information
courtesy of
Margaret Wilson Allen*

WITHROW, WILBUR M.

Wilbur M. Withrow, a resident of Rutherford County, died in service of his country during World War II.[1]

---

[1]*The Heritage of Rutherford County North Carolina, Volume I, 1984.* (Editors include William B. Bynum, Katherine Sanford Petrucelli, Joyce S. Tate, Beatrix Ramey, Glenn James, Max G. Padgett, Mabel Doggett, Scott Withrow, and Nancy Ellen Ferguson) Winston-Salem, North Carolina: The Genealogical Society of Old Tryon County incorporated in cooperation with The History Division, Hunter Publishing Company, 1984.

WOMACK, JOHN
November 20, 1944

Private First Class John Womack died of wounds received in action, according to a message received here. He was first reported as wounded on November 17, 1944.

Private First Class Womack (1917-1944) entered the U.S. Army in July of 1940. He spent twenty-two months in foreign service, mostly in the British West Indies, and returned to the United States. He was sent overseas about six months ago. He was a graduate of the class of 1938 at Cliffside High School.

Private First Class Womack was survived by his parents, Mr. and Mrs. H. G. Womack, of Cliffside; his wife, Mrs. Gladys Allen Womack of Forest City; and the following brothers and sisters: Mrs. Glenn McKinney, Mrs. Ola Pearson, Mrs. Frank Aldridge, and Miss Nell Womack, all of Cliffside.

Private First Class Womack was a radio operator for an Infantry Regiment. He was 27 years old on November 7, 1944. (*Forest City Courier*, December 14, 1944)

A memorial service was held Sunday for Private First Class John Reid Womack at the Cliffside Baptist Church. He died November 20, 1944, of wounds received in action three days prior to his death. A son of Mr. and Mrs. H. G. Womack of Cliffside, he married Miss Gladys Allen of Forest City on November 19, 1943. (*Forest City Courier*, February 1, 1945)

Photo courtesy of <u>Daily Courier</u>, Forest City, North Carolina, and James R. Brown, Publisher

AFTERWORD

I was born in March of 1943, and you–my father, Corporal Arthur Fred Price–died in Germany on December 28, 1944. You were the victim of the land mine you had just set. Although I was less than two years old when you died, I DO know you.

P. R. Price, my grandfather and "Pop", made sure I knew my "upbringings." When I was on Pop's hip or at his side, he never failed to introduce me to the customers in his dry goods store at the Rutherford/Cleveland County Line.

Anita Price Davis (3 months) "propped up" for photo for her father to take with him overseas.

"This is the Toodle! Her father was killed in service."

My grandfather Plato Rollins Price spoke these words in the same manner each time. He always swallowed hard after saying them, and he always paused for a moment to allow the customer to think about his statement. I knew these words made my Pop sad, but I knew he was proud of you–and of me. Until his death, Pop (February 22, 1887-November 4, 1976; Bethel Baptist Church Cemetery, Ellenboro) helped keep your memory alive.

He told others about you throughout his life. More than 30 years after your death he still introduced me as, "The Toodle, whose father was killed in service." He still swallowed hard after saying the words, and he still paused for a moment to allow the customer to think about his statement. He was still proud of you–and of me.

My mother never stopped loving you and remembering you. She told me everything about you. She told me how Grady Franklin–her cousin–brought you to meet her, Nell Gray Daves (May 25, 1923-February 2, 1998), for the first time; she remembered how you first saw her with a bee-bonnet on her head as she helped her father rob the hive. She told me how handsome you were and how you smiled at her embarrassment when her unexpected guests arrived.

Others have told me how beautiful my mother was and how much in love you two were. Victoria Luckadoo remembered how the young people in the area–you included–often pooled pennies to buy gasoline for Sunday afternoon rides; she laughed and said after you met my mother, you had no more time to ride around with the group.

Mother told me how you two were married on June 22, 1941, in Gaffney, South Carolina, and how you two spent your wedding night with Ruth and Ervin Grindstaff–

Nell Daves Price (Burns)

your sister and her husband (your employer). She told me about the beautiful white gown with blue stars that Aunt Ruth had laid on the bed for her to wear on her wedding night.

P. R. Price's Store Courtesy of Carolyn Grindstaff Barbee

Mother told how you often held her on your lap and sang "Melancholy Baby" to her. She told me how you later held me on your lap and sang "You Are My Sunshine" and "Tweedle O'Twill" to me. She told me how you sold your car nicknamed "Evalena" to pay the hospital for my delivery. She told me how you worked in the mica fields with your friend John Brooks and how you worked in Grindstaff's Store to provide for us. She told me of your love of reading and how you read me "the funnies," Tarzan, and comic books when I was just a few days old; she always laughed and said you enjoyed the comics as much as I did.

Carolyn Grindstaff Barbee, your niece, reminded me where you and my mother lived in relation to her home. She said she loved to ride her bicycle to visit with you and my mother–and later with me. She said she felt the happiness of our family when she came to our home on Cherry Mountain Street in Ellenboro.

Your nephew Boyce remembered spending Saturday nights with us and waking to the smells of the kerosene stove. Like mother, he recalled how eagerly you always opened the Sunday comic section and how you read the cartoons aloud to everybody—laughing all the while.

Boyce remembered that one night you allowed him to go on a date with you and mother. You ordered him a grilled pimento cheese sandwich and a Cherry Smash after the feature at the Romina Theater. Boyce still vows this was the best food he has ever eaten and can never be matched again.

You responded to Order Number 11756 and reported to City Hall, Forest City, on July 15, 1943, at 7:15 a.m. You were barely 19 (June 24, 1924-summer of 1943) when you left Mother and me with your parents. They were good to us, and my mother helped to "earn our keep" by assisting with the cooking, the cleaning, and the work in the store.

Mother was ecstatic when you came home on furlough. You two had your picture made together.

Mother kept every letter that you sent. When you wrote before Christmas of 1944 that you wanted her to buy a rocking horse for me, she did. I still have the letter, the horse, and a photograph of me on the horse, but I never had a Christmas with you.

Anita Price Davis with Horse "Bought" by Arthur F. Price, Christmas 1944

Your brother Falls William Price (July 12, 1918-), Company C, 423 Infantry Regiment, 106th Division (Golden Lion) spent some time with you on December 23, 1944, however. He was sitting in a restaurant in Liege, Belgium, when he looked up and saw you walking down

Photograph of Arthur F. (left) and Falls W. Price in Liege, Belgium, December 23, 1944

the street. It was a grand reunion! What a wonderful Christmas present for you both!

The two of you had your pictures made together and sent them home for your families to see. These are the last photographs ever made of you. The family still treasures them.

Your task in the Engineers, Uncle Falls explained, was to help throw up a bridge across the Rhine. It was a few days later that the terrible accident occurred that your family stateside would receive with grief and horror.

My mother told me often of the dark, rainy day when the telegram arrived. She told me how she had boiled my diapers and hung them on the line that day. When she looked out later, they were lying in the red, wet

Carolina clay, and she had to start all over again. She told me how she had just put me down for a nap and how she had just begun washing her beautiful, blond hair when the knock came at the door. It was a man with a telegram. Her first words were, "Oh! Arthur must be coming home!" The telegram, however, said you had been killed.

In the movies, an army officer often arrives to give the bad news. A chaplain sometimes accompanies the messenger; sometimes even a doctor arrives. My mother, however, was the only adult in the home to receive that horrible news. She was in a house with no phone, no car, and no close neighbor to run to through the downpour. She told me how she cried and held on to me–the last bit of you she had–as the messenger drove away.

Your body was interred in the United States Military Cemetery, Margraten, Holland, Plot P, Row 1, Grave 20. We thought of you often. You were in a foreign country, but you were with those who were grateful for your sacrifice.

Some time after your death, a handsome, older friend came to call on Mama and me. Robert Ewart Burns–and others who knew you–later said he had promised you that he would care for us if you did not return. And care for us he did! He married my Mama and dearly loved both of us as only a mature bachelor in his 40's could do. He understood a work ethic, duty, honor, unselfishness, responsibility, and love. He taught them to me–at your request. He spoke of you always with respect, and he never was jealous of your memory. Later he modeled these priceless

Robert Ewart Burns
(May 8, 1904-November 25, 1984,
Bethel Baptist Church Cemetery)

traits for my son, whom you could not have foreseen–or maybe you did.

Even before the end of World War II, Forest City began to recognize the sacrifice of its servicemen. The Lions Club sponsored the Memorial Avenue Project. A tree was planted as a memorial for those who gave their lives in World War II. Beginning at the edge of the Square and moving eastward along United States Highway 74 a silver maple was planted for each soldier, marine, sailor, or auxiliary service person who died in service. The list when the Memorial Avenue was begun surpassed 100; those numbers would increase. The project brought state and national attention to the city. (*Forest City Courier*, April 26, 1945)

On July 5, 1945, the *Forest City Courier* was able to report that a small, white pine marker was being placed at each tree on Memorial Avenue. We visited your tree often. (The Lions Club replaced the wooden plaques with bronze tablets after the War was over.)

At the request of my grandmother, you (Corporal Arthur Fred Price, 34778984, of Company B, 172 Engineers [Combat] Battalion) were brought to the United States aboard the United States Army Transport *Haiti Victory* in 1949. The remains of 90 other North Carolinians who lost their lives during World War II were returned at that time. You were originally in a temporary military cemetery in Holland. (*Forest City Courier*, March 18, 1949) You were buried in Grave 886, Section B of the National Cemetery in Salisbury, on April 27, 1949.

I remember the ceremony well. I remember sitting with my mother in a folding chair and how she screamed aloud with each volley of shot. We all sent flowers to honor you even though we knew that in the military cemetery the flowers would not remain overnight. We were proud to be with you again. We wanted you to know. My mother made my photograph at your grave; I always regretted having smiled.

At the end of the war, when the federal government announced that scholarships might be available for children of veterans who died on active duty, my mother wrote to the Veteran's Administration at once. She made a copy of her letters to the local Veteran's Administration and to the VA in Washington, D.C. The letters, which she kept as her written contract, informed them, "Anita is going to use that scholarship. Go ahead and reserve her scholarship for her. She is five-years-old and will be entering college in 1961. (Actually I "skipped a grade" and entered college a year early.) Her father gave his life, she is smart, and she will use the education to advantage. Her father was taken from her; I do not want this taken from her grasp. Reserve her place."

So you see, college was always a given for me–because of you. There was no other choice. I was always told, "Study hard. You'll need this in college." I never considered whether I would go to college; I just had to decide where I would go.

By graduating from high school a year early, by overloading each college semester, by attending college year round, I was able to secure my BS, MA, and part of my doctorate with the legacy you left for me.

When I hear others telling of the sacrifice they made to get their college education, I sympathize. Yet I know in my heart that you made the supreme sacrifice–unknowingly and without choice, but still the supreme sacrifice: you gave your life for me and for our world.

As I have entered the college classroom each morning during my 33 years of teaching–38 if you count the 5 years in public school–two thoughts go through my head. First, I pray that I will do my best. Second, I give thanks for what I have in my life.

When I use my gift of education, when I look at your picture, when I see your eyes in the face of my son, I know you are not gone. Others, too, still remember you after more than half a century.

My mother kept you always in her heart and mind. Your brothers and sisters pledged to my grandparents that they would keep your memory alive to their children and their grandchildren. They've kept their pledges! At a recent family gathering, parents and grandparents called young children I had never seen before to my side. The adults would say, "This is Toodle." The youngsters would immediately respond, "You're Arthur's girl." Even though my hair is gray, and even though I have a son of my own, I am still defined by you.

Your grandson (Robert Eric Davis, July 21, 1972) continues to make his mark as an attorney who married another brilliant attorney (Stacey Marie Campbell, April 14, 1972). You would be proud of their loving home.

You gave your family and your land all you had; you gave yourself. We are grateful. We will not forget you or the others who made the supreme sacrifice.

As a reminder of those who gave their lives, there is now a Rutherford County Memorial Garden comprised of the bronze plaques origi-nally placed beside the trees on Memorial Avenue. The cemetery is behind the "old" Cool Springs School on Main

Street. That Memorial Garden—orchestrated by Nancy and Harold Stallcup and others—ensures that your sacrifice and the sacrifice of the 148 other World War II servicemen who died on duty will be remem-bered. Other wars have added to the markers in the Memorial Garden.

This book *Real Heroes: Men from Rutherford County Who Made the Supreme Sacrifice During World War II* is my tribute to you. Had I waited another ten years, the information on many of the "real heroes" might have been impossible to find. Recording their information with yours is my way of saying, "Thank you" to all of our "real heroes."

BIBLIOGRAPHY

Boatner, Mark M., III. *The Biographical Dictionary of World War II.*
Novato, California: Presidio Press, 1996.

Bradley, James. *Flags of Our Fathers.* New York: Bantam Books, 2000.

Brown, James R., Publisher. *Daily Courier, Forest City, North Carolina.*
(Brown gave me the right to use photos, obituaries, and news stories
from *The Spindale Sun, The Rutherford County News,* and *The Forest
City Courier.*)

Griffin, Clarence. *History of Rutherford County, 1937-1951.*
Asheville, North Carolina: The Inland Press, 1952.

http://www.usarotc.com/medals/sm/htm

Lemmons, Sarah McCulloh. *North Carolina's Role in World War II.*
Raleigh, North Carolina, 1964.

*Pictorial History of the Second World War: A Photographic Record of
All Theaters of Action Chronologically Arranged.* (10 Volumes)
New York: Wm. H. Wise and Co., Inc., (1942-1949).

Silverstone, P.H. *U.S. Navy Warships of World War II.*
New York: Doubleday, 1968.

This photo of a perfect P-38 formation flying over France is one of the most beautiful pictures of the war. (U.S. Air Force)

A soldier moves "on the double" past still-burning German vehicles.
(U.S. Army)

***General of the Army, Douglas MacArthur, and Fleet Admiral, Chester
W. Nimitz stride across the deck of the U.S.S. Missouri to complete
the final act of Japan's formal surrender on September 2, 1945.***
(U.S. Navy)

This painting by Lieutenant Colonel J. J. Capolino, U.S. Marine Corps, is from an Associated Press photo by Joe Rosenthal. Rosenthal's photo of the flag-raising on Iwo Jima is the outstanding picture of World War II.
(U.S. Marine Corps)